The
CREAKY KNEES
Guide

OREGON

The
CREAKY KNEES
Guide

THE **80** BEST EASY HIKES

Seabury Blair Jr.

SASQUATCH BOOKS
SEATTLE

Printed in the United States of America
Published by Sasquatch Books
Distributed by PGW/Perseus
15 14 13 12 11 10   9 8 7 6 5 4 3 2

Cover photograph: © Eric1513 / Dreamstime.com
Cover design: Rosebud Eustace
Interior design and composition: Rosebud Eustace
Interior photos: Seabury Blair Jr. (except pages 18 and 81: photos by Marlene Blair, and pages 21 and 24: photos courtesy of Oregon State Parks)
Interior maps: Erin Stuart / maps created using TOPO! software © 2010 National Geographic Maps / Topo maps produced by the U.S Geological Survey

Library of Congress Cataloging-in-Publication Data

Blair, Seabury.
  The creaky knees guide Oregon : the 80 best easy hikes / Seabury Blair Jr.
    p. cm.
  Includes index.
  ISBN-13: 978-1-57061-627-3
  ISBN-10: 1-57061-627-2
  1. Hiking--Oregon--Guidebooks. 2. Oregon--Guidebooks. I. Title.
  GV199.42.07B6 2010
  796.5109795--dc22

                              2010003926

Important Note: Please use common sense. No guidebook can act as a substitute for experience, careful planning, the right equipment, and appropriate training. There is inherent danger in all the activities described in this book, and readers must assume full responsibility for their own actions and safety. Changing or unfavorable conditions in weather, roads, trails, snow, waterways, and so forth cannot be anticipated by the author or publisher, but should be considered by any outdoor participants. The author and publisher will not be responsible for the safety of users of this guide.

Sasquatch Books
119 South Main Street, Suite 400
Seattle, WA 98104
(206) 467-4300
www.sasquatchbooks.com
custserv@sasquatchbooks.com

Contents

The Umpqua Dunes make for unique hiking in Oregon.

Hikes at a Glance

Stroll in the Park

NO.	HIKE NAME	RATING	BEST SEASON	KIDS	DOGS
1	Astoria River Walk	🚶🚶	Summer	✔	✔
2	Airport Dike Trail	🚶	Summer		✔
3	Fort to Sea Trail South	🚶🚶🚶	Summer	✔	✔
7	Battery Russell Loop	🚶🚶	Summer	✔	✔
8	Seaside Promenade	🚶🚶🚶🚶	Winter	✔	✔
10	Arcadia Beach	🚶🚶🚶	Summer	✔	✔
26	Old Columbia River Highway, Viento State Park	🚶	Winter	✔	✔
28	Rowena Plateau	🚶🚶🚶	Spring	✔	
40	Trillium Lake Loop	🚶	Summer, fall	✔	✔
65	Mount Howard	🚶🚶🚶🚶🚶	Summer	✔	✔
77	Eastbank Esplanade Loop, Portland	🚶🚶🚶🚶	Summer		✔
78	Minto-Brown Island Park, Salem	🚶🚶🚶	Summer		
80	Pre's Trail, Eugene (walkers)	🚶	Summer		

Easy Walk

NO.	HIKE NAME	RATING	BEST SEASON	KIDS	DOGS
5	Fort Stevens Beach, Peter Iredale	🚶🚶🚶	Summer	✔	✔
6	Coffenbury Lake Loop	🚶🚶	Spring	✔	✔
12	Beverly Beach	🚶🚶🚶	Summer	✔	✔
13	Boice Cope North	🚶🚶🚶🚶	Summer	✔	✔
14	Boice Cope South	🚶🚶	Summer	✔	✔
16	Whalehead Cove	🚶🚶🚶🚶	Summer	✔	✔
21	Ponytail Falls	🚶🚶🚶	Spring	✔	✔
22	Gorge Trail 400, Eagle Creek to Bridge of the Gods	🚶	Winter	✔	✔
25	Lancaster Falls	🚶🚶	Spring		✔
31	Deschutes River Trail	🚶🚶	Spring, fall	✔	✔
32	Deschutes Rail Trail	🚶🚶🚶🚶	Spring	✔	✔
33	Wildwood Recreation Area	🚶	Spring	✔	✔
46	Lost Lake Loop	🚶🚶	Fall	✔	✔
50	South Breitenbush Gorge	🚶🚶🚶	Spring	✔	✔
51	Crown Lake	🚶🚶🚶	Summer, fall	✔	✔
58	West Metolius River	🚶🚶🚶	Fall	✔	✔

63	Paulina Lake	🚶🚶🚶🚶	Summer, fall		✓
72	North Fork John Day Wildnerness	🚶🚶🚶🚶	Summer	✓	✓
74	John Dellenback Trail, Diamond Lake	🚶🚶🚶🚶	Fall		✓
79	Riverfront Park, Corvallis	🚶🚶🚶	Spring	✓	✓

Moderate Workout

NO.	HIKE NAME	RATING	BEST SEASON	KIDS	DOGS
4	Fort to Sea Trail North	🚶🚶	Summer	✓	
11	Cape Lookout	🚶🚶🚶🚶🚶	Winter, spring		✓
17	Latourell Falls Loop	🚶🚶🚶	Spring	✓	✓
20	Triple Falls	🚶🚶🚶	Spring	✓	✓
23	Metlako Falls	🚶🚶🚶🚶	Spring, fall		✓
24	Dry Creek Falls	🚶🚶	Spring	✓	✓
27	McCall Point	🚶🚶🚶🚶	Spring		
29	Mosier Tunnels	🚶🚶🚶🚶	Spring, fall	✓	✓
30	The Dalles Riverfront Trail	🚶🚶🚶	Spring, fall	✓	✓
34	Salmon River Trail	🚶🚶	Spring, summer		✓
35	Pacific Crest Trail North, Lolo Pass	🚶🚶	Summer		✓
37	Bald Mountain Loop	🚶🚶🚶🚶	Summer	✓	✓
38	Mirror Lake	🚶🚶🚶🚶	Summer, fall	✓	✓
39	Zigzag Canyon	🚶🚶🚶🚶	Summer, fall	✓	✓
41	Twin Lakes	🚶🚶🚶	Summer, fall	✓	✓
42	Barlow Road	🚶	Fall		✓
43	Palmateer Loop	🚶🚶	Fall		✓
44	Timothy Lake West	🚶🚶🚶🚶	Summer, fall	✓	✓
45	Timothy Lake North	🚶🚶🚶	Summer, fall	✓	✓
47	Tamanawas Falls	🚶🚶🚶	Fall	✓	✓
49	Dark Lake	🚶🚶🚶	Summer, fall	✓	✓
52	Triangulation Peak	🚶🚶🚶🚶	Summer, fall		✓
54	Square Lake	🚶🚶🚶🚶	Summer, fall		✓
55	Wasco Lake	🚶🚶🚶🚶	Summer, fall		✓
56	Canyon Creek Loop	🚶🚶🚶🚶🚶	Summer, fall		✓
59	Deschutes River Reach	🚶🚶	Spring, fall		✓
60	Deschutes River Trail West	🚶🚶	Fall		✓
62	Smith Rock	🚶🚶🚶	Spring, fall		✓
64	Chimney Rock	🚶🚶	Spring, fall		✓
66	Dutch Flat Trail	🚶🚶	Summer, fall		✓
68	Black Lake	🚶🚶🚶	Summer, fall		✓

70	Crawfish Basin Trail	🚶🚶🚶	Summer, fall	✔	✔
71	Crawfish Lake	🚶🚶	Summer, fall		✔
73	Timothy Meadows	🚶🚶	Fall, summer		✔

Prepare to Perspire

NO.	HIKE NAME	RATING	BEST SEASON	KIDS	DOGS
9	Tillamook Head	🚶🚶🚶🚶	Summer		✔
15	Umpqua Dunes	🚶🚶🚶🚶🚶	Spring	✔	✔
18	Angel's Rest	🚶🚶🚶🚶🚶	Fall, summer		✔
19	Multnomah Falls	🚶🚶🚶🚶	Spring		✔
36	Pacific Crest Trail South, Lolo Pass	🚶🚶🚶	Summer		✔
48	Tilly Jane Loop	🚶🚶🚶🚶🚶	Summer		✔
53	Marion Lake	🚶🚶🚶🚶	Summer, fall	✔	✔
61	Todd Lake	🚶🚶🚶🚶	Summer, fall		✔
69	Hoffer Lakes Loop	🚶🚶🚶🚶	Summer, fall	✔	✔
75	Cleetwood Cove	🚶🚶🚶	Fall, summer		✔
80	Pre's Trail, Eugene (joggers)	🚶	Summer		

Knee-Punishing

NO.	HIKE NAME	RATING	BEST SEASON	KIDS	DOGS
57	Black Butte	🚶🚶🚶🚶🚶	Fall		✔
67	Elkhorn Crest	🚶🚶🚶	Summer, fall		✔
76	Mount Scott	🚶🚶🚶🚶🚶	Fall, summer		

ACKNOWLEDGMENTS

My wife, Marlene (aka B. B. Hardbody), deserves much more than thanks for her patience, encouragement, and help in completing this guide. The trails wouldn't be there were it not for the hard work of National Park and U.S. Forest Service staff and the many volunteers who keep them in such good condition. We all owe them our gratitude.

I'm also grateful to the many good people I met while hiking in Oregon, particularly Linda Starr of the Multnomah Athletic Club, who suggested a number of the Central Oregon hikes in this book. Thanks also to The Ladies and Two Guys, who joined me on regular hikes that kept me in good enough condition to walk the trails outlined here. The Ladies and Two Guys are nearly as old—older in some cases—as I am. The Ladies: Jean Cornwell, Karen Johnson, Tamae Johnson, Joyce Kimmel, Gayla Perini, Ann Richey, and Linda Weinacher. The Two Guys: Gary Larson and Jim Drannan, the Gnarly Dude.

Thanks, finally, to Gary Luke, Kurt Stephan, and all of the folks at Sasquatch Books.

INTRODUCTION

I bumped into a fellow wilderness pedestrian while hiking above Timberline Lodge a couple of years ago, and while I panted like an ancient steam donkey and tried to catch my breath, he chatted along as if he didn't notice I was sweating a new tributary to the Sandy River. He was talking about how great it was to get outdoors in Oregon, and how few places in America served up such a tasty variety of things to do. "Why, the other day I did an S and S," he said.

"What's that?" I wanted to know.

"I went skiing in the morning up here, then drove down to Hood River and went sailing."

Indeed, Oregon is a place where you can hike on a glacier in the morning and catch a salmon in the afternoon. You can walk through forests that were saplings hundreds of years before Columbus landed on America's shores and the next day, wander through a trackless desert. You can climb sand dunes where it rains more than 75 inches a year or walk sandscapes where it rains less than 7 inches. You can look into a clear lake that was once a steaming volcano and miles away trek beside the lava fields that spit from Mount Mazama.

The wildlife is just as diverse as the climate and geology. Whales swim off the coast, coyotes and foxes cry in the dry canyons of the east, elk herds cruise the high meadows and ridges of the Blue Mountains, and now, the cry of the wolf can be heard in Oregon again.

One thing is common throughout this state: the pedestrians who ply the wild pathways from west to east and north to south are pretty much the same. They all know and love the country at their back door—be it forest or flatland, mountain or meadow, desert or river. In checking the trails for this guide, I met a guy with two artificial knees headed up Tom, Dick, and Harry Mountain, and the Wednesday Women Hikers, a group of fiftyish ladies practically running up the Mirror Lake Trail. They told me about their favorite hikes and where I might find one of my own.

From the Mazama climber on the Twin Lakes Trail to the backpacker on the Pacific Crest Trail, the people who hike the wild pathways of Oregon will tell you the same thing: walking is the best thing you can do for your soul and your body. Being surrounded by the beauty around this neck of the woods certainly helps, and age and physical condition are simply not as important as getting outside to see what surprises Mother Nature plans for us. It is in that spirit that I offer this guide to all of you.

Sooner or later, we all realize that "easy hike" is a relative term. What might be an easy hike when you are 22 years old, so full of vim and vigor, is not likely to merit that same adjective when you are 52 and the vigor has morphed to varicose veins. So while the 80 hikes outlined in this guide are all labeled "easy," you are likely to find yourself at least once wondering if I am already senile. If you feel—as I often do when trying to keep up with my wife, B. B. Hardbody—like a leaking hydration pack, I'll be happy. In fact, if you don't curse me at least once while sweating up a hill or limping back to the trailhead, I have failed in my mission. Don't be fooled by the title. Unless you are a retired Olympic athlete or can still jog a dozen miles in under an hour, you'll find a hike or two in this guide to keep your heart rate up and your lungs sucking harder than a Dyson.

I've been lucky in my more than six decades on this planet to stay healthy enough to keep walking, and in those years, I have met hundreds of people on the trail who aren't as fortunate as me. My recent hiking partners include a woman who speeds through the forest on an artificial hip and a 74-year-old man with a steel joint where his knee used to be. They leave me a quivering mass of flab and sweat on the trail. I have also walked with younger folk who wonder why they can't keep up with that old bald man with the bouncing belly he calls Stummick. The important thing, it seems to me (and Stummick), is that regardless of age or physical condition, you try one of the trails outlined here. You'll be accompanied by beauty and solitude found in few other places on earth.

USING THIS GUIDE

The beginning of each trail description is intended to give you quick information that can help you decide whether the specific day hike is one that interests you. Here's what you'll find:

TRAIL NUMBER AND NAME

Trails are numbered in this guide following the main highway corridors in four geographic regions in the state: the Oregon Coast, the Columbia Gorge, Mount Hood, and Central Oregon. I've also included a dozen hikes in the more distant part of the state, including the Wallowas, Elkhorn Crest, and the Crater Lake region, as well as four of the best urban trails in Oregon.

OVERALL RATING

Rating these hikes was difficult for me. "In the first place," I asked the very wise and generous editor, "why would anyone want to take a hike I rate with only one star? A guidebook should only outline hikes that are worth taking, not dung-heap trails you wouldn't recommend to a psycho killer."

He replied: "True, but you must distinguish between the very best trails—with five stars—and the trails that aren't quite so good—with one to four stars." The trails that really suck (and I paraphrase here because editors are much too refined to use that term) won't be outlined here. Some hikes may not be as good as others, but they are all better than the ones that really bite.

Another problem I had was attempting to be objective in rating the trails. I'm a pushover for hikes above timberline, where the wildflowers wave in gentle summer breezes, where mountains claw the clouds, where cooling snowfields linger through summer. So I may have rated these trails higher than you might rate them.

If you're a hiker who loves walking along rattling rivers or past forested lakes, or padding on rain-forest trails softened by mosses, I'd suggest you add one star to every lowland hike and subtract one star from every alpland hike in this guide.

Finally, objective criteria like trail conditions, trail length, and obstacles such as creek crossings can affect the overall rating. On the other hand, you can forget all that junk and just take my word for it.

DISTANCE

The distance listed is round-trip, exclusive of any side trips mentioned along the way. If these excursions off the main trail are longer than 0.2 mile or so, I'll mention it in the description of the hike.

In an effort to prove that trails indeed are getting longer as I grow older, I pushed a bike wheel equipped with a cyclometer around some of the trails in this guide and packed a GPS on others. I learned to my disappointment that trails aren't getting longer—although there are notable exceptions—and that I might have equipped myself better by carrying my own oxygen supply instead of a bloody heavy bike wheel or a GPS unit that is allergic to fir and pine forests.

HIKING TIME

This is an estimate of the time it takes the average hiker to walk the trail round-trip. Since none of us are average hikers, you may feel free to ignore this entry.

For the most part, I calculated the pace on the trail to be between 1.5 and 2 miles per hour. I assumed the pace might slow on trails with significant elevation gain or loss and tried to err on the conservative side. It's my hope that many of you will wonder what sort of trail slug came up with such ridiculously long hiking times.

ELEVATION GAIN

This is a calculation of the total number of feet you'll have to climb on the trail. Don't assume, as one fool early in his hiking days did (I have since learned better), that all of the elevation will be gained on the way to your destination. Some of these trails actually lose elevation on the way and gain it on the return, or alternately gain and lose elevation along the way. It has always been a source of wonder to me that on a round-trip hike, you always gain the same amount of elevation that you lose.

HIGH POINT

This is the highest point above sea level you'll reach on any given hike. In cases like the ocean beach walks, it is always at the trailhead.

EFFORT

This was another tough one for me. I've been hiking for so many years it is a task to remember what it was like to take some of these hikes as a novice. My good friend Grizzly Hemingway once turned back from a hike after encountering a footlog that was too high to cross—a log I had forgotten scared the pee out of me the first time I crossed it, too.

So again, I tried to be conservative in judging the effort it would take to finish each hike. Where previous guides discussed overall difficulty of the trail, I thought the energy expended to hike out and back might be more meaningful. A hike might be difficult, for example, if you had to walk that footlog, but the rest of the trail could be flat as a pancake griddle, requiring no more effort than a stroll in the park. Thus you'll find the following categories:

A **Stroll in the Park** will serve up few, if any, hills to climb and is generally between 1 and 3 miles long round-trip, a hike suitable for families with small children.

On a hike rated as an **Easy Walk,** you might expect to find longer, but still gently graded, hills and trails around 2 to 4 miles long round-trip.

A hike described as a **Moderate Workout** would be one with longer grades and elevation changes greater than about 500 feet from beginning to high point, hikes between 3 and 5 miles long round-trip.

A hike rated **Prepare to Perspire** is one that will make your deodorant fail you, no matter your excellent physical condition. It will have sustained steep climbs of at least 1 mile, with elevation gain and loss greater than 1,000 feet, and is about 4 to 6 miles long round-trip.

A **Knee-Punishing** hike is one that will challenge your physical abilities beyond what you might expect you can accomplish, one that will send you rushing to the anti-inflammatory shelf in your medicine cabinet upon your return.

BEST SEASON
Here is my suggestion for the months I think you'd most enjoy this hike, as well as whether the path will be free of snow throughout the year.

PERMITS/CONTACT
This entry will tell you whether you need a Northwest Forest Pass and who to contact for information. In the case of Crater Lake National Park, I've included general fee information. Hikers who are fortunate enough to have been on earth 62 years or longer qualify for an America the Beautiful Senior Pass, which, at $10 for life, gets you onto just about any federally managed trail and gives you half-price camping at National Forest campgrounds.

MAPS

I've tried to include the USGS quadrangle maps for every hike in the guide, plus Green Trails maps where available. I've not listed, but recommend, the several Geo-Graphics Maps for many Oregon hiking regions.

TRAIL NOTES

Here are some regulations specific to each hike you'll most likely want to know: whether leashed pets can accompany you; whether you'll encounter mountain bikes, equestrians, or ATVs on the trail; whether your children might like this hike. If there are circumstances about the hike you might like to know, such as whether you'll fry if you hike the trail in summer, I'll mention it here.

THE HIKE

This is an attempt to convey the feel of the trail in a sentence or two, including the type of trail and whether there's a one-way hiking option.

GETTING THERE

Here's where you'll either find out how to get to the trailhead or, if I've screwed up, become hopelessly lost. You'll learn the elevation at the trailhead and—assuming my GPS didn't sniff any firs or pines—the coordinates for the trailhead.

As I mentioned, all of the hikes are organized according to the major highway corridors you'll follow to get to the National Forest or Park roads leading to the trailhead. I've tried to indicate starting points along those corridors, such as cities or towns, or major highway junctions.

THE TRAIL

Here's where you'll get the blow-by-blow, mile-by-mile description of the trail. I've tried to stick to information your feet will find useful and apologize if, every now and then, I look up to recognize an awesome view or rhapsodize about something absolutely without redeeming social or cultural value. I'm guessing you'll recognize these features without much coaching.

GOING FARTHER

This is an important category in this guide, because many of you might find some of these hikes too easy, while others will be ready to turn around before they reach my recommended spot. For that reason, I've tried to include a suggestion for extending every hike from the same trailhead—or from a nearby trailhead that can be accessed before your heart rate decreases or your joints stiffen.

BE CAREFUL

It is all too easy on a warm, sunny day on the trail to forget all of the stuff you ought to be carrying in your pack. Day hikers, especially, are likely to leave that extra fleece sweater or that waterproof, breathable parka in the trunk. Some folks even forget that First Essential—a hiking partner.

Never hike alone.

Virtually all the time, day hikers who forget one or two of the basic rules for safe wilderness travel return to the trailhead smiling and healthy. No trail cop is going to cite you for negligent hiking if you have only nine of the Ten Essentials, or if you hit the trail without registering or telling someone where you're going.

I dislike preaching safety—if you looked in my pack on a good-weather day hike, you might find my extra clothing consists of a spare do-rag and my map clearly shows the hike I took last week. Perhaps the only weighty argument anyone can make to convince another day hiker to follow the rules for safe travel in the out-of-doors is to remind them of the annual, avoidable tragedies that occur because hikers ignore those rules.

First—no matter the distance or difficulty of the hike—please carry the Ten Essentials in your pack. With no apologies to those credit card people: don't leave home without them.

- A topographic map of the area.

- A compass, and the ability to use it in conjunction with the map. While excellent aids to navigation, portable GPS units are no substitute for a compass that does not require batteries or satellite reception.

- Extra clothing, which should consist of a top and bottom insulating layer and a waterproof, windproof layer. A hat or cap is absolutely essential: mountaineers will tell you that when your feet are cold, put on your hat. It works.

- Extra food. To avoid grazing on my extra food, I try to pick something I would only eat if I were starving. Stuff like freeze-dried turnips or breakfast bars that taste like pressed sawdust fire starters. In fact, some of my extra food can be used as emergency fire starters.

🚶 A flashlight with extra batteries and bulbs. I carry a headlamp because it allows me to swat at the moths that fly into the light without dropping the bloody flashlight. Many of these lights have spare bulbs built in. Lithium batteries, though more expensive, make excellent spares because their shelf life is longer than yours.

🚶 A first-aid kit. You can buy these already assembled, and they are excellent. Consider one thing, however: the type of injury that is likely to incapacitate a day hiker will probably be different than that suffered by a backpacker. If your first-aid kit doesn't include wraps for sprains, add an ankle support, at the very least. Blister treatment for day hikers is another essential.

🚶 Matches in a waterproof case. Although butane lighters are often carried as a substitute, both altitude and temperature can affect their performance.

🚶 A fire starter. Candles work well, along with a variety of lightweight commercial fire starters.

🚶 A pocket knife. In addition to the all-important corkscrew, my Swiss Army knife has 623 blades, including a tiny chain saw.

🚶 Sunglasses and sunscreen.

In addition to these items, most day hikers never hit the trail without toting some toilet paper in a plastic bag and perhaps some type of bug repellent on summer hikes. A loud emergency whistle is a lightweight addition. Binoculars may help you find your route if you become lost and are worth the weight simply for watching wildlife.

WEATHER

Every region in Oregon demands we pay attention to a different facet of the weather. On the coast, a dry change of clothing in the pack or car is always a good idea because rain can sneak up on you. In the dry canyons of the Deschutes, an extra liter of water would be a better idea.

No matter where you're hiking, learn to read the clouds and wind and learn the general rules that may keep you safer or more comfortable. Winds from the southwest often bring storms. Northerlies often herald better weather. Afternoons in the high country are more likely to be stormy. I like to think of Mother Nature as a schizoid who is most often a friendly, generous old lady who bakes cookies and bread for you, but when you least expect it, puts on a goalie's mask and whacks at you with an icicle or lightning bolt.

So be prepared, Scouts.

WATER

You'll find plenty of opportunities to refill your water bottle on many of the hikes outlined in this book, especially on the wet west side of the Cascades. Treat all water as if it were contaminated, although this is not as great an issue in Oregon wilderness as it is often suggested by those who might be held liable if you were to contract a waterborne illness. The most worrisome problem with the water might be a little critter called *Giardia lamblia*, which can give you a case of the trots that you'll never forget. The most noticeable symptom of giardiasis is "explosive diarrhea." Need I say more? I think not.

Thankfully, there is an easy way to assure that the water you take from mountain streams and lakes is safe to drink. When used properly, filter pumps eliminate at least 99.9 percent of *Giardia* and other dangerous organisms from the water. A recent and far more convenient addition to filter pumps, especially for day hikers, is a relatively inexpensive water bottle equipped with its own filter. You simply fill the bottle from the stream (taking extreme care not to contaminate the mouthpiece or drinking cap), drop the filter into place, and screw on the top, and you're ready to drink filtered water. Perhaps the most effective water treatment is with chemicals such as iodine; the trade-off is processing time.

WILDLIFE

The first time I saw a black bear, a half mile from the trailhead, I snapped a shaky picture of it and considered shedding my pack on the spot so it would eat my lunch and not bother making lunch of me. Since that time, I have come to regard animals and plants that share the wilderness as benign, for the most part.

Day hikers certainly needn't fear black bears, but they must realize these are wild animals that can cause serious injury if provoked. Research indicates that a black bear attack—though extremely rare—may often be more serious than an attack from a grizzly. Respect a bear's personal space, in short, and never get between a cub and its mother. If you encounter a black bear on the trail, make certain it knows you're there by addressing it in a calm voice (it will probably run off at this point), give it a wide berth, and count yourself fortunate for seeing it. Some few bears have learned that humans carry food in their packs, but this is a far greater concern to backpackers, and you'll find warnings or closure signs at the trailhead.

A greater potential danger might be from cougars. Until recently, I've regarded myself lucky to have seen a cougar once in the Cascade Mountains and discovered I was once tracked by an unseen cougar through 5 miles of snow. But there is growing evidence to suggest that day hikers should treat cougar sightings as extremely dangerous encounters with predators who, it appears, may sometimes hunt humans for food. Shortly before setting out to check the trails in an earlier guide, I read Jo Deurbrouck's and Dean Miller's excellent book *Cat Attacks*. It convinced me that—though the odds of being attacked by a cougar are on the order of winning the lottery while being struck by lightning—I should be more aware of the animals to whom the wilderness belongs, particularly the ones that are quite capable of hunting you down and killing you.

Trailhead signs will tell you how to respond if you are confronted by a cougar on the trail. Generally, you must face the animal down. Don't turn your back on it or bend down to get something to throw at it. Shouting may help. Barking like a dog may send the animal off into the woods. But most importantly: Maintain eye contact at all times.

Most unsettling is the fact that the majority of cougar attacks upon humans don't occur as a result of the kind of encounter described above. Most people who were attacked by cougars in the past decade—attacks have increased significantly in the past 10 years—were struck from behind and were not aware of the cougar's presence until the attack.

How can a hiker defend against such an attack? Given that the odds of an encounter are extremely remote and an attack less likely still, author Deurbrouck suggests hikers simply be aware of places where cougars are most likely to wait in ambush. She says that while trail-running, she tries to think like a deer, the cougar's main prey. In other words, be watchful of banks above the trail and places where the trail rounds hillside corners. In most cases, cougars attack from ambush, above and behind their prey.

Above all, cougar attacks of the past decade have given greater weight to the unbreakable rule against solo hiking. When attacking, cougars appear to be so focused on their prey that they completely ignore other people. Even when companions open a big can of whup-ass on that kitty, they are most likely to escape a retaliatory attack. Those attacked by cougars can be saved by companions who most likely won't suffer injury from the animal—and I'm hoping that is by far and away more than you want or will ever need to know about cougars.

Less dangerous but more common hazards to day hikers might include stinging and biting pests like yellow jackets—particularly in late summer and early autumn—blackflies, mosquitoes, and deerflies. Liberal doses of insect repellent can take care of the mosquitoes and deerflies but probably won't keep those nasty yellow jackets away. My technique for protection from yellow jacket stings is to send my hiking partners ahead about 100 feet; if they get stung as they pass a nest, I wait until things settle down, then bypass the area carefully.

Poison oak and ivy grow in some areas, particularly on the east side of the state and Columbia Gorge, but are easily avoided by learning to identify the plants. A more common plant pest is stinging nettle, which grows along many trails on both the wet and dry side of the state, but it can be recognized and avoided most of the time.

Snakes are common on the sunny side of Oregon; you have only to keep a watch out for them to enjoy a safe, bite-free hike. If only I had taken that advice before I stepped on that snake a couple of years ago while ogling the hills for mountain sheep. Neither the snake nor I stuck around long enough to find out if either of us was poisonous.

A cave carved by the surf can be found on the beach at Whalehead Cove.

OREGON COAST

The Pacific Ocean shoreline in Oregon is indeed rare real estate, because it belongs to everyone. That a vast majority of its owners take such good care of it is evident from long stretches of clean and wild sand. Even heavily used areas where motorized vehicles are permitted are generally devoid of the mess found elsewhere, and that is testimony to the respect residents have for the property they own in common.

You might think, as some visitors do, that walking a beach or coastal trail can be pretty much the same north to south. Of course, that's not so. The hikes outlined here include precipitous cliffside views where whales play, dunes so inviting you may never reach the surf, and stately promenades past historic places first visited by white explorers only 200 years ago.

The walks suggested here follow the route of U.S. 101, the Oregon Coast Highway, as it winds south to the California border. The hikes are numbered beginning in the north, at Astoria.

OREGON COAST

1. Astoria River Walk

RATING	🚶 🚶
DISTANCE	5.0 miles round-trip
HIKING TIME	2 hours, 30 minutes
ELEVATION GAIN	Negligible
HIGH POINT	30 feet
EFFORT	Stroll in the Park
BEST SEASON	Summer; open all year
PERMITS/CONTACT	None/Astoria Parks and Community Services, (503) 325-7275
MAPS	USGS Astoria
NOTES	Leashed dogs welcome; good family walk; wheelchair accessible

THE HIKE

Join the local residents in a scenic walk at the mouth of the Columbia River, where seagoing ships come and go and winged wildlife is everywhere.

GETTING THERE

From the Astoria Bridge across the Columbia River, drive east on Marine Drive (U.S. Highway 30) through downtown to the trailhead at the Safeway parking area at Leif Erikson Drive, 25 feet above sea level. GPS trailhead coordinates: N46°11.991'; W123°46.621'

THE TRAIL

It would be difficult to apply the "urban trail" label to this excellent paved pathway along the banks of the Columbia River, simply because the views of the river speak more eloquently about the wildlife you'll see along the shore. Call the trail what you will, but make sure you add it to your list of walks along the splendid Oregon coast.

While the water side of the trail is great for watching birds, the youngsters—and oldsters, for that matter—might find the ever-changing marine traffic scene more interesting. You'll see huge cargo ships and van carriers, tugboats, and maybe even a cruise ship or two. Astoria is a busy seaport and the first stop in the marine highway that follows the

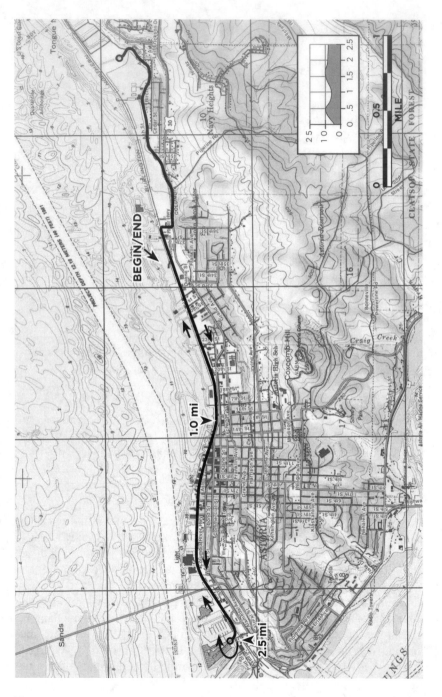

Astoria's River Walk features a maritime theme.

Columbia River to The Dalles and beyond. You can even find out what ships are coming and going, and what time they are expected to sail under the Astoria Bridge, by tuning to the local radio station.

Pick up the trail along the trolley tracks—which it parallels for about 2.0 miles—from the trailhead, and walk westerly along the river. This portion of the trail is paved the entire distance and is just about as flat as a trail can get. You'll pass the main downtown area of Astoria about halfway through your walk and, at **2.0** miles, you'll walk under the Astoria Bridge. The trail continues another 0.5 mile to the Port of Astoria.

GOING FARTHER
You can add another 2 round-trip miles to your hike by walking east on your return past the trailhead and following a primitive path that meanders east to Tongue Point.

2. Airport Dike Trail

RATING	🚶
DISTANCE	4.2 miles round-trip
HIKING TIME	2 hours, 15 minutes
ELEVATION GAIN	Negligible
HIGH POINT	25 feet
EFFORT	Stroll in the Park
BEST SEASON	Summer; open all year
PERMITS/CONTACT	None/Port of Astoria, (503) 325-4521
MAPS	USGS Warrenton
NOTES	Leashed dogs welcome

THE HIKE

Here's an easy walk that is sure to please birders and small aircraft fans alike. Look inland for the airplanes and toward the Columbia River for Mother Nature's aircraft.

GETTING THERE

From Astoria, follow U.S. Highway 101 south across the Youngs Bay Bridge to the Premarq Shopping Center just south of the bridge; turn left into the parking lot. The trailhead is just across the highway to the east, 25 feet above sea level. GPS trailhead coordinates: N46°09.848′; W123°53.660′

THE TRAIL

If you find yourself in Astoria and have only a few hours to get outside, the Airport Dike Trail offers a little more solitude than the Astoria River Walk (hike #1 in this guide). If there's a single problem with this hike, it's getting across U.S. Highway 101 to the trailhead. Plans call for a pathway at the west end of the trail along the Oregon Department of Transportation right-of-way, and a trailhead at the east end, but they were still plans as of the spring of 2009. A small gravel parking area at the east end is available, just off the U.S. Highway 101 business route.

Once on the trail, things quiet down and in 0.1 mile you'll cross the Adams Slough and stroll above the river and airport to the south—which, at 11 feet above sea level, has got to be one of the lowest airports in

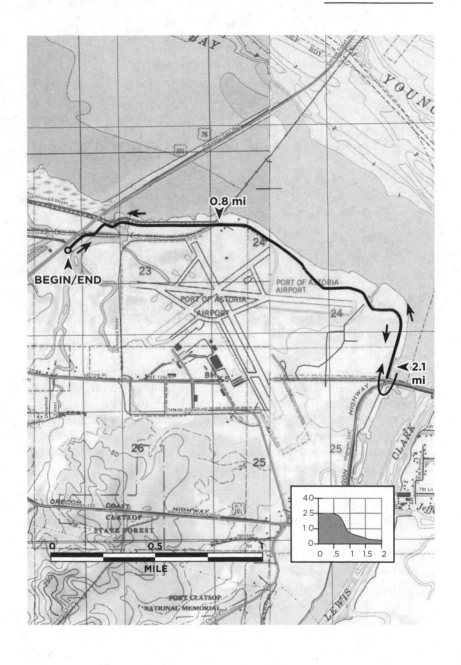

Priscilla and Modie the dog hike the Airport Dike Trail.

Oregon. While many coastal trails can get wet during the rainy season, drainage engineered into the dike assures your boots aren't likely to suffer muddy indignity. The surface of the trail is mostly grass.

The route makes a broad turn to the south about a mile from the trailhead, then turns sharply east into woods at the east end of the airport. It turns again to the south for 0.2 mile before jogging east to the eastern trailhead. This is your turnaround point.

GOING FARTHER

For a longer walk, you can follow a trail that leads west from the parking lot to the Skipanon Peninsula Trail, which follows the Skipanon River to its mouth in the Columbia River. Round-trip distance of this loop trail is about 1.8 miles.

3. Fort to Sea Trail South

RATING	🚶 🚶 🚶
DISTANCE	6.0 miles round-trip
HIKING TIME	2 hours, 30 minutes
ELEVATION GAIN	30 feet
HIGH POINT	45 feet
EFFORT	Stroll in the Park
BEST SEASON	Summer
PERMITS/CONTACT	None/Sunset Beach State Park, (800) 551-6949
MAPS	USGS Gearhart
NOTES	Leashed dogs welcome; great family walk

THE HIKE
This is the ocean-side portion of a historic route traveled by the Lewis and Clark Expedition to reach the Pacific coast from their coastal quarters at Fort Clatsop, long before U.S. Highway 101 bisected the path.

GETTING THERE
From Astoria, follow U.S. Highway 101 south to milepost 13 and turn left on Sunset Beach Lane and drive to Sunset Beach State Park. Look for the Fort to Sea Trail parking area and trailhead on the right, 15 feet above sea level. GPS trailhead coordinates: N46°05.959´; W123°56.225´

THE TRAIL
The Lewis and Clark Corps of Discovery spent the winter of 1805 at Fort Clatsop at the northern end of this trail in a dank and dismal rain forest, but you'll be walking the sandy beachside end of the trail. Though the route is among the oldest in the state, the trail itself is relatively new. Largely through the work of youth groups and volunteers, the trail was rebuilt after portions of it were wiped out by winter storms in 2008.

Begin by walking northeast, following gentle sand dunes where the rush and muffled hush of the surf will keep you company and shorebirds cry above. The trail here is mainly sandy soil and generally well drained, making it the more popular half of the trail in winter rains. You'll wind through beach woods where trees are sculpted by coastal winds, and at **0.7** mile from the trailhead you'll cross Neacoxie Lake on a footbridge.

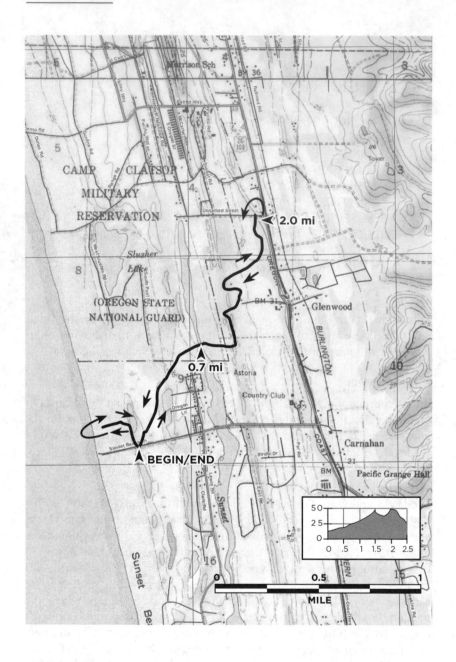

The south trailhead of the Fort to Sea Trail begins near Sunset Beach.

The path winds in and out of the woods and dunes near the edge of a golf course for another mile before turning to the east at a pedestrian underpass of U.S. Highway 101, your turnaround point. Return the way you came, then follow the 0.5-mile one-way path from the parking area to the wide Sunset Beach, an excellent picnic spot.

GOING FARTHER

Two options for extending your walk come to mind: following Sunset Beach to the south as far as your creaky knees and tides permit, or continuing to the northeast on the Fort to Sea Trail to Fort Clatsop. Choosing the second option would yield a round-trip hike of 13 miles, although in the summer you can ride a shuttle back to Sunset Beach.

4. Fort to Sea Trail North

RATING	👤 👤
DISTANCE	6.4 miles round-trip
HIKING TIME	3 hours, 30 minutes
ELEVATION GAIN	220 feet
HIGH POINT	260 feet
EFFORT	Moderate Workout
BEST SEASON	Summer; open all year
PERMITS/CONTACT	None/Lewis and Clark National Historic Park, (503) 861-2471
MAPS	USGS Gearhart
NOTES	Dogs prohibited on trail; good family walk; portion of trail is wheelchair accessible

THE HIKE

Follow the route the Lewis and Clark Corps of Discovery took from their winter quarters of 1805 at Fort Clatsop to the ocean beach, a historical hike if ever there was one.

GETTING THERE

From Astoria, follow U.S. Highway 101 south to Fort Clatsop Road, turn left, and follow the signs to the Fort Clatsop Visitor Center. You'll be asked for an fee ($3 in 2009) upon entering the area. Trailhead parking is adjacent to the visitor center, 20 feet above sea level. GPS trailhead coordinates: N46°08.059´; W123°52.866´

THE TRAIL

Imagine Captain William Clark and Sergeant John Ordway returning to Fort Clatsop in the summer of 1806. It would have been a different scene than that of the soggy, cold April when the Corps of Discovery began the long return journey east.

Clark: "Let's hit the beach, bro. It's too hot and muggy here."

Ordway (eagerly): "Yessir, yessir! Too damn hot to work, heh?"

So they don their scratchy wool swimsuits and Ordway—due to his lowly rank—grabs a giant beach umbrella and a couple of kites, and the two tromp through the woods to the ocean. They follow the trail they

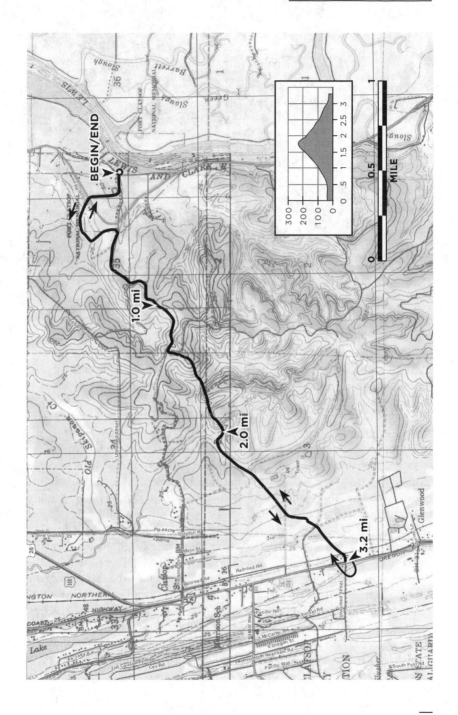

The northern trailhead of the Fort to Sea Trail begins at a kiosk at Fort Clatsop National Memorial.

blazed months before, climbing over Clatsop Ridge to Sunset Beach. In those days, of course, they didn't have to pay an entrance fee at the Fort Clatsop Visitor Center.

Today you can follow in their steps, walking a significantly better path than the one the Corps slogged more than 200 years ago. Parts of the route today are on plank bridges and turnpikes, thanks largely to volunteers and youth groups who rebuilt the trail following the severe winter storms of 2008. Yet despite all the modern improvements, Mother Nature conspires with Old Man Winter to install a few slippery and muddy patches along the way to the beach.

You'll begin a gentle climb into a lush forest of hemlock and spruce to the crest of Clatsop Ridge, where you may be able to glimpse the Pacific Ocean through the forest. Elk and deer, as well as smaller critters like the winter wren, populate this section of forest. (As you probably know, the winter wren is the tiny bird that in springtime sings a song at least 4,000 times longer than its wingspan.) Crest the ridgetop at 1.8 miles, then begin a descent 2.0 miles from the trailhead into deeper forest.

Emerge from the woods in another mile to wooded pastureland punctuated by a number of small lakes where birds (and birders) are likely to be spotted. The birders are the ones with expensive binoculars. In another 0.2 mile, you'll arrive at an underpass at U.S. Highway 101, your turnaround spot.

GOING FARTHER

If you'd like to extend your walk, you can continue another 3 miles to the ocean at Sunset Beach. That would be a round-trip hike of 13 mostly flat miles. In the summer, you can ride a shuttle back to Fort Clatsop Visitor Center from the Sunset Beach trailhead, 0.5 miles from the ocean.

For a shorter extension, return to the Visitor Center and follow the 1.5-mile one-way walk along the Netul River.

5. Fort Stevens Beach, *Peter Iredale*

RATING	🚶 🚶 🚶
DISTANCE	3.6 miles round-trip
HIKING TIME	2 hours
ELEVATION GAIN	20 feet
HIGH POINT	25 feet
EFFORT	Easy Walk
BEST SEASON	Summer; open all year
PERMITS/CONTACT	Day Use Permit required/Oregon State Parks, (800) 551-6949
MAPS	USGS Warrenton
NOTES	Leashed dogs welcome; good family hike

THE HIKE

Follow an ocean beach north from the ship wreckage that ran aground more than 100 years ago to picnic spots in the sands overlooking the mouth of the Columbia River.

GETTING THERE

From Astoria, follow U.S. Highway 101 south to signs pointing to Fort Stevens State Park and turn right, following the signs through Warrenton and Hammond to the park. Turn right at the campground entrance to the park, where you can purchase a Day Use Permit ($3 in 2009). Drive past the intersection with the campground road to the day use area adjacent to the beach at the wreckage of the *Peter Iredale*. The trailhead, 15 feet above sea level, is sometimes covered by beach sand, especially in the winter. GPS trailhead coordinates: N46°10.689′; W123°58.749′

THE TRAIL

"May God bless you, and may your bones bleach in the sands." So toasted Captain H. Lawrence, commander of the good ship *Peter Iredale*, after the 285-foot steel barque ran aground on October 25, 1906. In fact, the skeleton of the ship can be seen off the Pacific Ocean beach to this day, one of the most accessible shipwrecks to be found anywhere on the coast. At low tide you can walk to the ship's rusting ribs sticking from the sands.

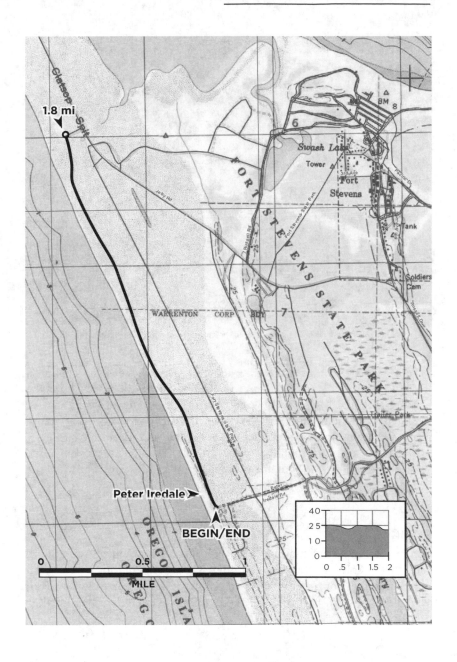

The wreck of the *Peter Iredale* is one of the sights on the beach walk north at Fort Stevens State Park.

Your hike north along the fine beach of Fort Stevens State Park is likely to begin with a visit to the wreckage, about 100 yards from the parking area and trailhead. Beyond, more than 2 miles of beach can be explored, with views out to sea of marine traffic approaching the mouth of the Columbia River, all manner of shorebirds, and incredible sunsets.

If you tire of beachcombing, you can return along the Kestrel Dune Trail above the sands. Your turnaround point is 1.8 miles north on the beach, at an equestrian parking area and a trail leading east to Trestle Bay.

GOING FARTHER

You can continue north along the beach for nearly 2 miles to the South Jetty of the Columbia River, where there's a viewing platform and beach access parking. For great wildlife-watching, follow the Trestle Bay Trail 1.1 miles, one-way, to a wildlife viewing blind overlooking Swash Lake.

6. Coffenbury Lake Loop

RATING	🚶 🚶
DISTANCE	3.6 miles round-trip
HIKING TIME	2 hours
ELEVATION GAIN	30 feet
HIGH POINT	50 feet
EFFORT	Easy Walk
BEST SEASON	Spring; open all year
PERMITS/CONTACT	Day Use Permit required/Oregon State Parks, (800) 551-6949
MAPS	USGS Warrenton
NOTES	Leashed dogs welcome; good family hike

THE HIKE

Bird and wildlife watchers will appreciate this springtime walk around Coffenbury Lake, a nice picnic spot only a short distance from the Pacific Ocean.

GETTING THERE

From Astoria, follow U.S. Highway 101 south to signs pointing to Fort Stevens State Park and turn right, following the signs through Warrenton and Hammond to the park. Turn right at the campground entrance to the park, where you can purchase a Day Use Permit ($3 in 2009). Drive past the intersection with the campground road to the day use area adjacent to the beach at the wreckage of the *Peter Iredale*. The trailhead, 15 feet above sea level, is sometimes covered by beach sand, especially in the winter. GPS trailhead coordinates: N46°10.689′; W123°58.749′

THE TRAIL

It might seem strange to some folks that, in view of all the surf and salt-water to the west, you would leave the parking area and head east along a paved trail away from the beach. This route meanders through groves of shore pine for 0.7 mile to the Coffenbury Lake day use parking area on the right. The path then circles the lake in a counterclockwise direction, serving up excellent opportunities to spy on the winged and four-footed

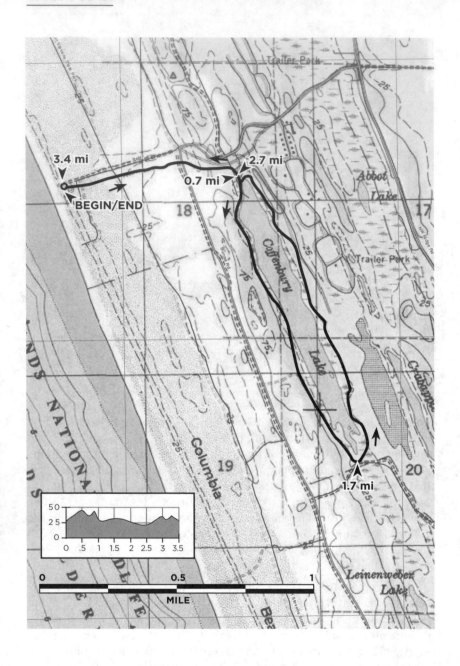

An easy trail circles Coffenbury Lake at Fort Stevens State Park.

natives who call the lakeshore forest home. Plan this walk in the early morning or evening for the best wildlife-watching.

To continue, hike to the south end of the Coffenbury Lake parking area and walk south along the lakeside. The path alternately winds in and out of the woods along the shore for 1.0 mile to the south end of the lake, where you'll turn on an old road and circle the marsh at its southern end. Look for the trail to the left leading along the eastern shore of the lake and follow it north past picnic and swimming areas to the day use parking area, **2.7** miles from the trailhead. Campers and visitors at Fort Stevens State Park prefer the warmer and wind-sheltered water of the lake for swimming.

Follow the trail from the Coffenbury day use area back to the Peter Iredale parking area, 0.7 mile.

GOING FARTHER

Several choices for extending your hike present themselves: walk the beach to the north past the wreckage of the *Peter Iredale* or follow the foot or bike trails leading to the historic Fort Stevens gun batteries. Round-trip hikes of more than 4 miles can be taken from a trail junction just west of the Coffenbury Lake day use area on the return from the loop around the lake.

7. Battery Russell Loop

RATING	🚶 🚶
DISTANCE	2.4 miles round-trip
HIKING TIME	1 hour, 30 minutes
ELEVATION GAIN	30 feet
HIGH POINT	60 feet
EFFORT	Stroll in the Park
BEST SEASON	Summer
PERMITS/CONTACT	Day Use Permit required/Oregon State Parks, (800) 551-6949
MAPS	USGS Warrenton
NOTES	Leashed dogs welcome; good family hike

THE HIKE

Follow a forested pathway past portions of the gun emplacements that guarded the entrance to the Columbia River, some dating back to the Civil War.

GETTING THERE

From Astoria, follow U.S. Highway 101 south to signs pointing to Fort Stevens State Park and turn right, following the signs through Warrenton and Hammond to the park. Turn right at the campground entrance to the park, where you can purchase a Day Use Permit ($3 in 2009). Drive past the intersection with the campground and Coffenbury Lake roads to a road leading right to the day use area at the Battery Russell area, then turn right to the Battery Russell parking area, 25 feet above sea level. GPS trailhead coordinates: N46°11.643′; W123°58.504′

THE TRAIL

You'll probably take longer on this hike than your normal walking pace, since you'll likely want to stop and explore the gun battery just off the trail to the right as you begin the loop trail to the south. Battery Russell was one of several gun emplacements designed to fire 10-inch-diameter shells at enemy ships trying to enter the Columbia River. The first guns were placed at the northern end of Fort Stevens in 1863 and 1864 to defend the river entrance from British and Confederate raiders.

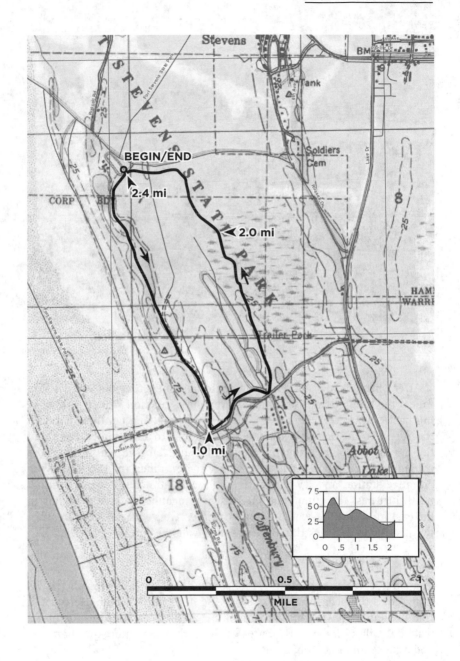

The Western Battery is among the gun emplacements at Fort Stevens State Park and overlooks the Columbia River.

After checking out the concrete buildings and commander's station, follow the forested path south for 0.3 mile to a junction with a path leading back toward the historic area. Stay right here, and continue through the forest to a junction with the trail leading to Coffenbury Lake and the beach, 1.1 miles from the trailhead. Turn left and walk above the campground entrance road, then follow the entrance road east past the entrance station and RV dump station to pick up the footpath leading north just past the dump station. This trail meanders above wetlands to the east for a wildlife-watching opportunity. After walking 1.0 mile, turn left just before a pedestrian overpass and walk west to the trailhead.

GOING FARTHER
You can add another historic 1.4 miles, one-way, by following the paved trail across the pedestrian overpass to the north for 0.8 mile. Here you'll find a wildlife viewing blind overlooking Swash Lake; beyond the blind, walk 0.6 mile to the historical area of the park, where more gun batteries and a museum are the main attractions.

8. Seaside Promenade

RATING	𝕏 𝕏 𝕏 𝕏
DISTANCE	3.6 miles round-trip
HIKING TIME	2 hours
ELEVATION GAIN	Negligible
HIGH POINT	15 feet
EFFORT	Stroll in the Park
BEST SEASON	Winter; open all year
PERMITS/CONTACT	None/Seaside Visitors Bureau, (888) 306-2326
MAPS	USGS Tillamook Head
NOTES	Leashed dogs, bicyclists, inline skaters welcome; excellent family walk; wheelchair accessible

THE HIKE

This is the granddaddy of all of Oregon's best easy walks and a model for communities looking to bring natural splendor to the most possible visitors.

GETTING THERE

Follow U.S. Highway 101 to Seaside and turn west on 12th Street. Follow 12th Street to its end at a big parking area at the north end of the promenade, 15 feet above sea level. GPS trailhead coordinates: N46°00.074'; W123°55.621'

THE TRAIL

Seaside—as anyone who has visited there will tell you—is built for pedestrians, and the best way for pedestrians to see the community is to follow the Seaside Promenade as it stretches 1.8 miles south along the Pacific Ocean beach. Once a boardwalk, the promenade was paved with concrete in 1920 and has attracted generations of families ever since.

The first and most obvious feature of this walk is the fact that no buildings or residences are located on the west side of the walkway. That is because the entire coastline of Oregon is publicly owned and ocean-front homes are restricted to an area behind the public beaches. Though popular any time of the year, winter might be the best season to walk the promenade to avoid crowds and watch the surge of the surf.

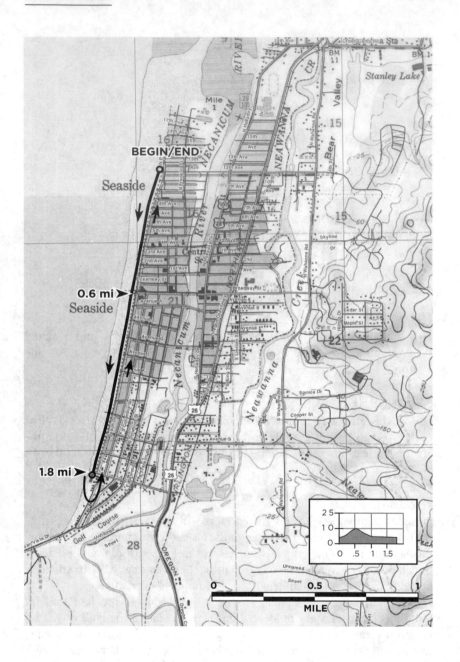

Walk in the footsteps of Lewis and Clark on the Seaside Promenade.

It is difficult any time of the year to avoid snapping up an elephant ear pastry downtown, or visiting the aquarium, or stopping at any of the other Seaside attractions along the way. Those temptations are likely to slow your pace. One spot not to be missed is the Lewis and Clark Salt Works, located about a block east of the promenade on Avenue U.

GOING FARTHER
The best way to extend your walk is to follow the beach north or south from the ends of the concrete promenade, as far as knees and tides permit. The beach to the north is probably more interesting.

9. Tillamook Head

RATING	🚶 🚶 🚶 🚶
DISTANCE	5.4 miles round-trip
HIKING TIME	3 hours, 30 minutes
ELEVATION GAIN	900 feet
HIGH POINT	1,200 feet
EFFORT	Prepare to Perspire
BEST SEASON	Summer; open all year
PERMITS/CONTACT	None/Oregon State Parks, (800) 551-6949
MAPS	USGS Tillamook Head; Tillamook Head National Recreation Trail topographic map
NOTES	Leashed dogs welcome

THE HIKE

It's a strenuous climb to one of the best viewpoints along the north coast to Tillamook Head, where you can see pretty much all the way to Hawaii—or at least to the point where it is difficult to tell the ocean from the sky.

GETTING THERE

From U.S. Highway 101 in Seaside, turn west on Avenue U to South Edgewood Street, then turn left and follow Edgewood to its junction with Ocean Vista Drive; follow Ocean Vista south to Sunset Boulevard, then follow Sunset Boulevard to its end. The trailhead is just opposite condominiums, 300 feet above sea level. GPS trailhead coordinates: N45°58.367'; W123°57.484'

THE TRAIL

Most hikers arrive at Tillamook Head from Ecola State Park at the southern end of the trail, but if you're cheap like me (I actually prefer the term "thrifty"), you'll avoid paying for the day use permit by parking at the Seaside trailhead. You'll exercise more, but you'll save enough to buy an elephant ear pastry in Seaside to reward yourself.

The trail begins with crossing a seasonal creek, then starts climbing immediately up a heavily wooded ridge for almost a quarter mile, giving no rest. You'll then turn toward the south and begin a gentler climb to

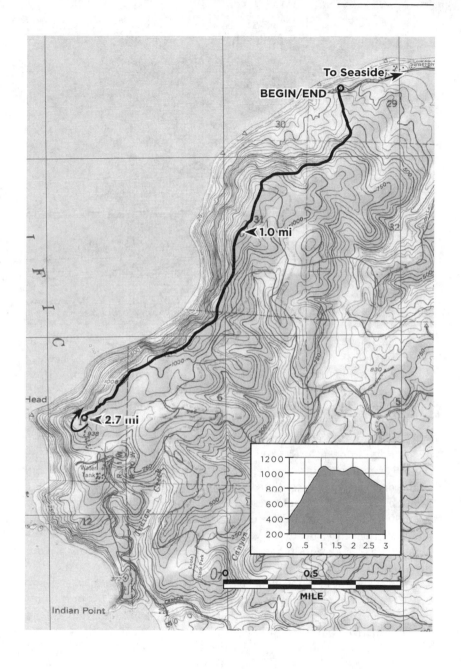

Tillamook Head stretches above the Seaside surf.

the first dramatic ocean viewpoint, carved from the forest **1.0** mile from the trailhead. This might be the best turnaround point for families with small children, because the view doesn't get any better until you reach Tillamook Head, another 1.7 miles distant.

To continue, follow the trail over a crest and contour along the rim of the ridge in deep forest. You should be able to hear the surf pummel the hillside, about 1,000 feet below, but you'll only get peekaboo views of the ocean. The trail continues in a southwesterly direction for a mile through the typical coastal forest of Sitka spruce, cedar, and hemlock. At **2.7** miles from the trailhead, you'll arrive at the Tillamook Head view-point with ocean vistas to the west, north, and south, as well as the Til-lamook Rock Lighthouse, one the oldest lights in Oregon. This is your turnaround point.

Beyond, the route drops in steep switchbacks and another 5.0 miles to Ecola State Park, where the Lewis and Clark Corps of Discovery traveled to get whale blubber from native fishers. "Ecola," say the tour guides, is a Native American word for "whale."

GOING FARTHER

It's 8 miles, one-way, to the Ecola State Park trailhead, making it an attractive alternative to parties who can park a vehicle at each trailhead, then swap keys at a halfway picnic spot.

10. Arcadia Beach

RATING	🚶 🚶 🚶
DISTANCE	3.4 miles round-trip
HIKING TIME	2 hours, 30 minutes
ELEVATION GAIN	30 feet
HIGH POINT	30 feet
EFFORT	Stroll in the Park
BEST SEASON	Summer; open all year
PERMITS/CONTACT	None/Oregon State Parks, (800) 551-6949
MAPS	USGS Tillamook Head, Arch Cape
NOTES	Leashed dogs welcome; good family walk

THE HIKE

Here's a good hike to get up close and personal with surging surf, followed by a nice walk for beachcombers and wildlife-watchers.

GETTING THERE

Drive 5 miles south on U.S. Highway 101 from Cannon Beach and turn right into the trailhead at Hug Point State Wayside, 300 feet above sea level. GPS trailhead coordinates: N45°49.725′; W123°57.612′

THE TRAIL

The walk along Arcadia Beach from Hug Point State Wayside is generally less crowded than other strands near Cannon Beach, because the uplands aren't nearly so crowded with houses. Try to time the hike with a low tide for better beach walking.

Begin by following stairs to the beach and turn north along the shore, where you'll pass a low point of land into a shallow cove surrounded by rock cliffs. There you'll find a waterfall and caves sculpted by waves in the rock. Beyond, you'll find the rough stage road blasted out of rock at Hug Point, 0.5 mile from the trailhead. You'll be only a few feet above the surf, and it's a good place to get a feel for the power of the Pacific Ocean.

Continue walking north as the rock of Hug Point turns to the wide sands of Arcadia Beach. You can follow the beach for 1.2 miles to Arcadia

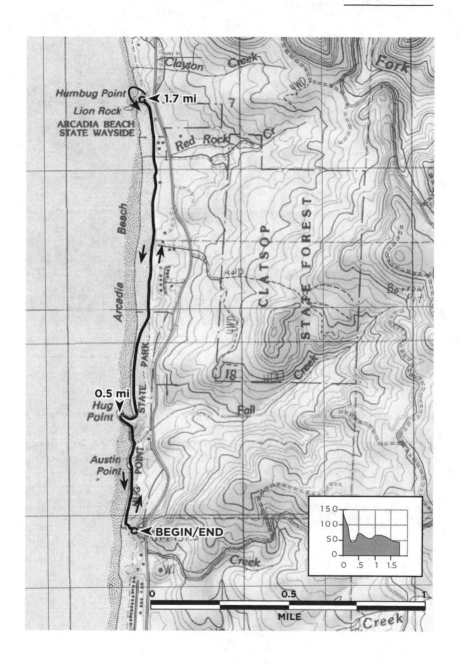

The hike from Hug Point ends here, at Arcadia Beach.

Beach State Wayside, crossing Red Rock Creek 1.1 miles from the trail-head.

GOING FARTHER
At low tide you can round Humbug Point, just beyond Arcadia Beach State Wayside, and continue about another mile, one-way, to the south end of Cannon Beach at Silver Point. Hikers seeking a longer walk can also trek south from Hug Point State Wayside by negotiating beach rocks for a short distance to a beach leading south to cliffs at Arch Cape. This route would add 1.7 miles, one-way, to your hike.

11. Cape Lookout

RATING	🚶 🚶 🚶 🚶 🚶
DISTANCE	4.2 miles round-trip
HIKING TIME	3 hours
ELEVATION GAIN	400 feet
HIGH POINT	800 feet
EFFORT	Moderate Workout
BEST SEASON	Winter, early spring; open all year
PERMITS/CONTACT	Day Use Permit required/Oregon State Parks, (800) 551-6949
MAPS	USGS Sand Lake
NOTES	Leashed dogs welcome; steep cliffside views

THE HIKE

The view from Cape Lookout is probably the best spot on the Oregon coast for watching gray whales, which could pass as close as 100 yards to the cape.

GETTING THERE

Drive 11 miles south of Tillamook on U.S. Highway 101 to the Sand Lake–Three Capes Scenic Loop and turn right. Follow the road to a stop sign and junction with the Sand Lake Road. Bear right and follow the road as it climbs to the Cape Lookout trailhead parking area on the left, 800 feet above sea level. GPS trailhead coordinates: N45°20.461'; W123°58.389'

THE TRAIL

Three trails begin within 100 feet of the trailhead. You'll want the central trail at each junction. The trail to the right drops in a little more than 2.0 miles to the Cape Lookout Campground, while the trail to the left descends to the beach south of the cape. So stay left at the first trail and right at the second. Beyond, there should be no confusion as the forested ridge narrows and there's actually only one way to go. After buying a Day Use Permit ($3 in 2009), you'll be ready to hit the trail.

If whale watching is your priority, the best time to take this hike is late December and early January, despite the often muddy and slippery

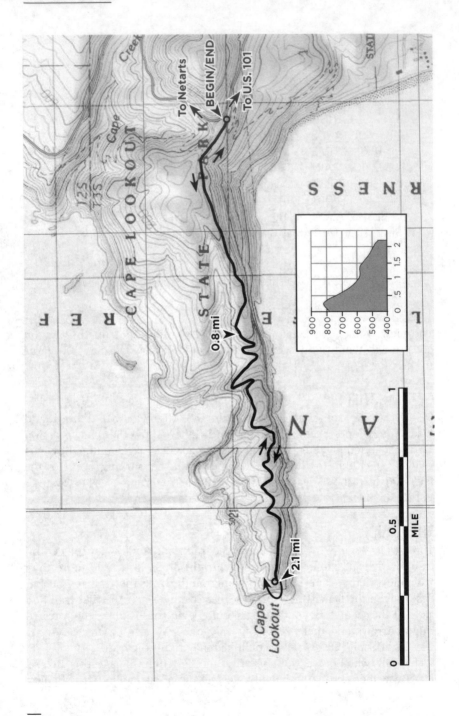

It's a long ways down to the south beach from the Cape Lookout trail.

conditions on the path. Whales migrate south in the early winter and north from mid-March to early April. It is estimated that an average of 22 whales pass the cape every hour during these periods. An estimated 200 gray whales spend the summer off the Oregon coast as well, so you might get lucky and see one then, too.

The view from the tip of the cape is spectacular any time of the year, though, so even if you don't make this hike during prime whale-spotting season, it is still a great walk. It isn't so steep or long as to discourage families with young children, but keep a sharp eye on the youngsters when the cliffs are close by. The trail descends gently for about 0.5 mile to the first viewpoint, where you can look down on the beaches south of the cape. It passes a plaque memorializing the victims of a plane crash in 1943, then turns to the north and drops gently to a second viewpoint where a fence guards against getting too close to the north-facing cliffs. You'll be standing 1.1 miles from the trailhead.

To continue, follow the trail south and walk through a thinning forest with views down to the ocean. The route now makes broad switchbacks as it meanders from the southern cliffs to the slightly less steep northern hillside. The turnaround is 2.1 miles from the trailhead, with vistas and exposed cliffs.

GOING FARTHER

For a real workout, hike the 3.6-mile round-trip trail to the beach south of Cape Lookout. That is a strenuous 850-foot climb down and back up from the beach. You can also hike the 2.4-mile one-way trail down to the campground.

12. Beverly Beach

RATING	🚶 🚶 🚶
DISTANCE	5.0 miles round-trip
HIKING TIME	3 hours
ELEVATION GAIN	Negligible
HIGH POINT	15 feet
EFFORT	Easy Walk
BEST SEASON	Summer; open all year
PERMITS/CONTACT	None/Oregon State Parks, (800) 551-6949
MAPS	USGS Newport North
NOTES	Leashed dogs welcome; good family walk

THE HIKE

One of the most popular beaches along the Oregon coast draws beach-combers, kite flyers, whale watchers, and campers. The broad beach invites hikers who can walk at least 5 miles with few obstacles to slow their progress.

GETTING THERE

Follow U.S. Highway 101 south about 22 miles from Lincoln City and turn left at the entrance to Beverly Beach State Park. Follow the signs to the day use parking area to the left. The trailhead is 15 feet above sea level. GPS trailhead coordinates: N44º43.763′; W124º03.407′

THE TRAIL

It's little wonder that Beverly Beach attracts the crowds. The sand is fine and firm, punctuated by the occasional field of rounded pebbles. It's an ideal spot for attempting to jog in slow-motion along the beach, listening to Vangelis's music from *Chariots of Fire* on your iPod. If you're in really good shape, you might even be able to hum along.

Begin by ducking under the U.S. 101 bridge and following Spencer Creek to the beach, then turn south and stroll as far as you want along the strand. The bluffs to the east begin crowding the beach at about 1.0 mile from the trailhead, but continuing south is not a problem at low tide.

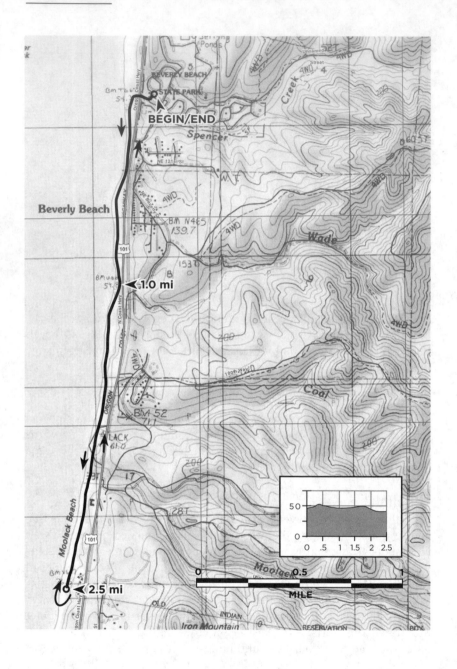

BEGIN/END

Beverly Beach

1.0 mi

2.5 mi

The U.S. Highway 101 bridge frames a view of the Pacific Ocean at Beverly Beach.

About 2.0 miles from the trailhead, you'll arrive at Moolack Beach, which is one of the more popular locations for agate hunting along the coast. Your turnaround point is 2.5 miles from the trailhead, at the southern end of Moolack Beach.

GOING FARTHER
You can hike the beach south to Yaquina Head and north to the headlands of Otter Rock. Yaquina Head is about 3 miles, one-way, from Beverly Beach; Otter Rock headlands is about 1 mile north.

13. Boice Cope North

RATING	🚶 🚶 🚶 🚶
DISTANCE	4.0 miles round-trip
HIKING TIME	2 hours, 30 minutes
ELEVATION GAIN	Negligible
HIGH POINT	29 feet
EFFORT	Easy Walk
BEST SEASON	Summer; open all year
PERMITS/CONTACT	None/Oregon State Parks, (800) 551-6949
MAPS	USGS Floras Lake, Cape Blanco
NOTES	Leashed dogs welcome; great family walk

THE HIKE

One of the most isolated beaches on the Oregon coast stretches north from Floras Lake more than 12 miles, the home of plovers that nest here. Upland portions of the beach are closed to protect the nesting areas.

GETTING THERE

Follow U.S. Highway 101 for 14 miles south of Bandon and turn right on the Floras Lake Loop Road. Then follow the signs to Boice Cope County Park, turning right after 1.1 miles at a junction and right again at 2.6 miles on Boice Cope Road. Drive 0.3 mile to the park and trailhead at the boat launch, 20 feet above sea level. GPS trailhead coordinates: N42°54.168´; W124°30.123´

THE TRAIL

The beach along the Pacific, both north and south from Floras Lake, is a great place to get away from crowds. You'll find an entirely different atmosphere from the popular Beverly or Cannon beaches, one where wildlife rules the waves and the sky.

Begin by crossing the bridge at the north end of Floras Lake, where hikers often leave their walking sticks against a tree for the next hiker, and hike west over low dunes to the ocean beach, 0.3 mile from the trailhead. If you're taking this walk in the spring, you'll see wild iris blossoming blue and strawberries hugging the sandy soil.

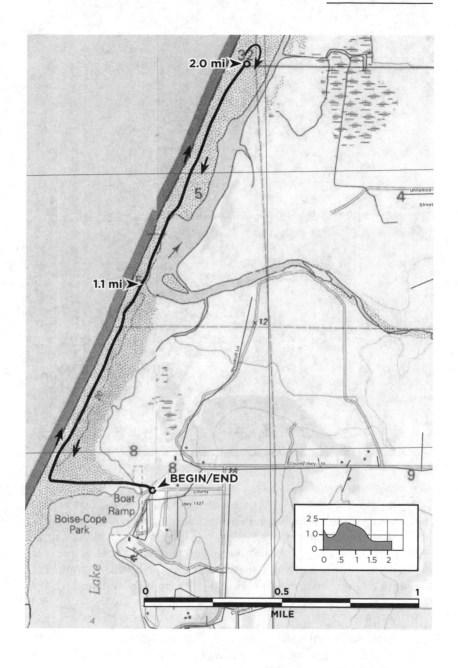

A collection of walking sticks awaits hikers on trails at Floras Lake and Boice Cope.

You'll pass a sign warning you to keep Fido on a leash and stay off the upland portion of the beach to protect nesting plovers before turning north on the beach. Stay along the low tide line on your walk, and at **1.1** miles from the trailhead you'll arrive at the south end of the point where the New River turns north and piles sand along the beach. Continue hiking north to your turnaround point, **2.0** miles from the trailhead.

GOING FARTHER

It's easy at low tide to walk north more than 5 miles, one-way, along the beach to make a daylong hike. Another option is to follow the beach to the south, hike #14 in this guide.

14. Boice Cope South

RATING	🚶 🚶
DISTANCE	4.6 miles round-trip
HIKING TIME	3 hours
ELEVATION GAIN	50 feet
HIGH POINT	50 feet
EFFORT	Easy Walk
BEST SEASON	Summer; open all year
PERMITS/CONTACT	None/Oregon State Parks, (800) 551-6949
MAPS	USGS Floras Lake, Cape Blanco
NOTES	Leashed dogs welcome; great family walk

THE HIKE

Walk south along a lakeshore where bird-watching and sailboarding are popular pastimes, then follow the beach at low tide south to views of Blacklock Point and a waterfall.

GETTING THERE

Follow U.S. Highway 101 for 14 miles south of Bandon and turn right on the Floras Lake Loop Road. Then follow the signs to Boice Cope County Park, turning right after 1.1 miles at a junction and right again at 2.6 miles on Boice Cope Road. Drive 0.3 mile to the park and trailhead at the boat launch, 20 feet above sea level. GPS trailhead coordinates: N42°54.168'; W124°30.123'

THE TRAIL

The hike along the beach south from Floras Lake begins with a bridge crossing at the north end of the lake. Just across the bridge, you'll likely find a collection of walking sticks leaning against a tree and interpretive signs regarding nesting plovers. Turn left along a faint trail that follows the shore of the lake, where posts mark the way to the south.

You'll follow the lakeshore for 0.9 mile to a junction that climbs away from the lake up the headlands toward Blacklock Point. Stay to the right here and drop to the ocean beach in another 0.1 mile. The beach should be hiked at low tide and the headlands draw closer to the surf at 1.5 miles from the trailhead.

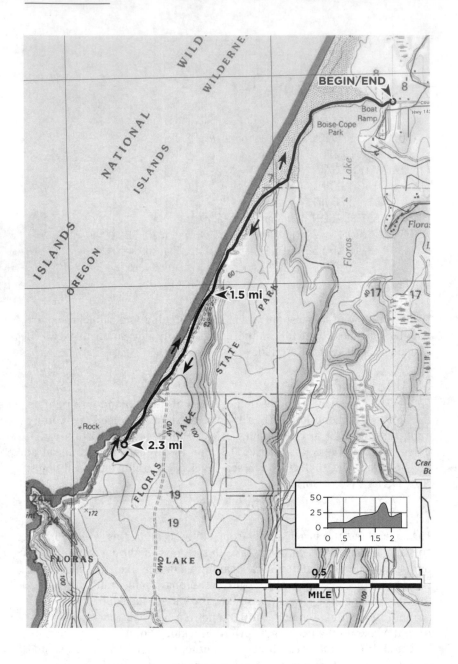

You might find yourself the only person on the beach walking south at Boice Cope.

Continue along the beach to a rocky point of land and the waterfall, 2.3 miles from the trailhead. This is your turnaround point.

GOING FARTHER

To extend your hike, you can return to the Blacklock Point trail junction and turn right. The trail climbs to the top of sandstone cliffs above the beach in coastal forest to a view from Blacklock Point, 3.9 miles, one-way, from the trailhead.

15. Umpqua Dunes

RATING	🚶 🚶 🚶 🚶 🚶
DISTANCE	4.4 miles round-trip
HIKING TIME	3 hours
ELEVATION GAIN	90 feet
HIGH POINT	120 feet
EFFORT	Prepare to Perspire
BEST SEASON	Spring
PERMITS/CONTACT	Northwest Forest Pass required/Oregon Dunes National Recreation Area, (541) 271-3611
MAPS	USGS Lakeside
NOTES	Leashed dogs welcome; great family adventure

THE HIKE

The ocean beach at the end of this hike is not the best part of the trek. In fact, if you're hiking with youngsters, you may not even reach the ocean and instead may spend all of your time playing on the dunes.

GETTING THERE

From Reedsport, drive 8 miles south on U.S. Highway 101 to the John Dellenback trailhead, just south of the Eel Creek Campground in Lakeside. The trailhead is 30 feet above sea level. GPS trailhead coordinates: N43°35.048′; W124°11.111′

THE TRAIL

The John Dellenback Trail in the Oregon Dunes National Recreation Area is utterly unlike any other hike in this guide. It is a walk through an alien landscape of incredible beauty, one that is sure to pack plenty of pixels in your digital camera. And pick a clear day for this walk; it is easy to get disoriented in the fog and you may find yourself enjoying an unscheduled compass practice.

Families with children should be prepared to stop at the first big dune and never get beyond that. These massive, moving mountains of sand are reminiscent of snow-covered winter slopes, complete with cornices and loose avalanches. Climbing the lee slopes of the dunes can be an

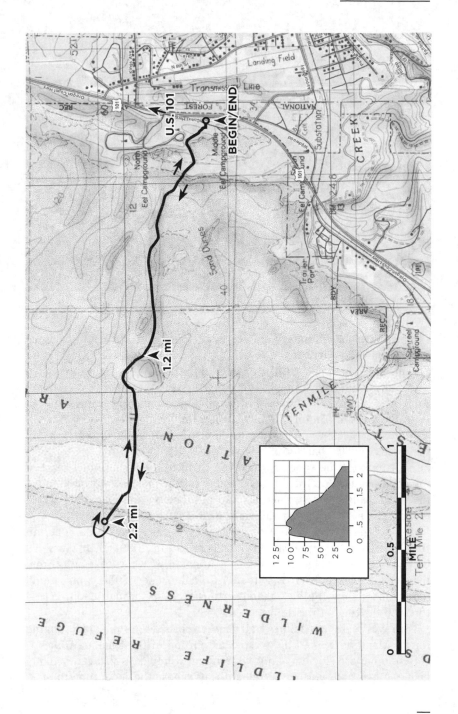

Poles mark the route across the Umpqua Dunes.

exhausting, shoe-filling experience, as I found out scrambling up the face of one dune.

The sand was unpacked like powder snow, and every step up resulted in a half step down. Though you can walk the dunes on more sound, solid sand, you'll miss the thrill of leaping off a dune or wading through shifting waves of trillions of silicon particles.

After nearly losing one of my low-cut hikers, I decided to follow my wife's advice: "Go barefoot!" shouted B. B. Hardbody from the top of a dune. I took off the shoes and carried them in the pack until I reached the approach trail on the return. It made for the most comfortable walking in the sand, but I strained my sad old flat feet and ended up unable to walk the next day. The pain was worth it.

If you don't have a Northwest Forest Pass, you can buy a daily permit from a self-issue station at the trailhead ($5 in 2009), then cross Eel Creek on a wide bridge. Stay left at a junction with a trail leading from the Eel Campground, cross a road leading to one of the campground loops, and follow the well-marked trail 0.5 mile through deep coastal forest to the edge of the dunes.

Turn west here and follow trail marker posts across the sand, aiming for an island of trees to the west. This portion of the Umpqua Dunes is closed to motor vehicles, so on the frequent windy days you can actually hear the hiss and whisper of the shifting sands. The ideal time to walk the dunes might be after a light rain, when you can follow areas of solid sand packed by the rain. Don't worry about encountering patches of occasional quicksand, which, despite its name, is notoriously slow.

Aim just to the left of the main island of trees to the west, passing the largest island of trees 1.2 miles from the trailhead. You should see a series of marker posts just west of the trees directing you to the north across a wet, marshy area, then climbing over the shoulder of the foredune to the ocean, 2.2 miles from the trailhead. Return the way you came.

GOING FARTHER

You'll find that dune-walking isn't as easy as you might think, but if you'd like to extend your hike, you can walk north or south along the beach until you've satisfied your lust for muscle pain or an ibuprofen overdose.

16. Whalehead Cove

RATING	🚶 🚶 🚶 🚶
DISTANCE	2.8 miles round-trip
HIKING TIME	2 hours, 30 minutes
ELEVATION GAIN	Negligible
HIGH POINT	20 feet
EFFORT	Easy Walk
BEST SEASON	Summer; open all year
PERMITS/CONTACT	None/Oregon State Parks, (800) 551-6949
MAPS	USGS Carpenterville, Brookings
NOTES	Leashed dogs welcome; good family walk

THE HIKE

This is a good beach hike at low tide, past a massive sea stack to a section of beach pocked by tidepools that invite exploration.

GETTING THERE

From Gold Beach, follow U.S. Highway 101 for 19.5 miles south to the Whalehead Cove Picnic Area. The 0.1-mile road down to the parking area is very steep and rough, but the parking area and trailhead are wide and flat, about 30 feet above sea level. GPS trailhead coordinates: N42°08.676′; W124°21.287′

THE TRAIL

The biggest adventure on this walk is finding a way across Whalehead Creek, just downhill from the trailhead. You may be able to find a driftwood crossing upstream, and the creek braids and shifts at its mouth so you might be able to rock-hop across. On the other hand, this is a beach walk: you're going to get wet sooner or later, so just get a firm grip on your trekking poles and wade right in.

Once across, walk the beach south past Whalehead Island, that big dark rock that—not surprisingly—resembles a whale's head. The beach is best walked at low tide, and just beyond you'll find a cave in the rock cliffs above the beach. Continue south along the beach where the sand shares the oceanfront with medium-sized cobbles rounded smooth by the

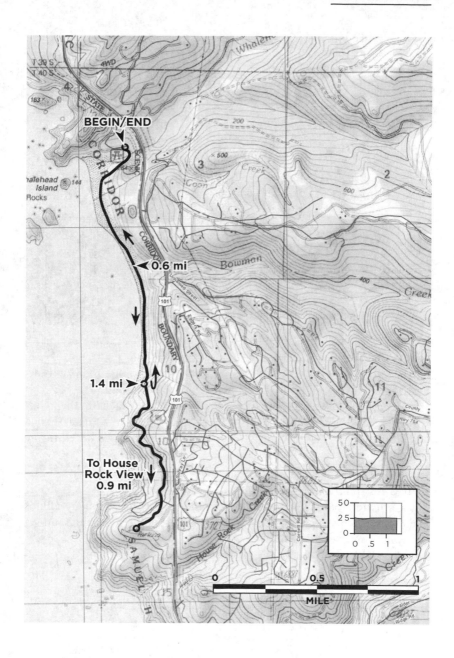

BEGIN/END

0.6 mi

1.4 mi

To House
Rock View
0.9 mi

MILE

0   0.5   1

The shape of the seastack at Whalehead Cove gives the place its name.

Pacific surf. The route crosses Bowman Creek at **0.6** mile from the trail-head, where a waterfall inland competes with the ocean vista.

Beyond, you'll wander on increasingly narrow beach to the point where the trail climbs inland, up a steep path through a forest shaped and stunted by frequent winds, **1.4** miles from the trailhead. Return the way you came.

GOING FARTHER

You can extend your hike by following the trail as it alternately climbs and drops, often steeply, to the House Rock Viewpoint, a 4.6-mile round-trip walk from the trailhead.

Hiking at Umpqua Dunes can be more challenging than you'd expect.

Triple Falls demonstrates the symmetry of Mother Nature.

COLUMBIA RIVER GORGE

The Gorge is a day-hiking treasure that I rediscovered six years ago, when I coaxed my old body and constant companion, Stummick, into walking all of the trails outlined here. Stummick—though he growled the entire distance—always finished in front of me.

Though the hikes in the Gorge are as diverse as hikes throughout the state, they share one similar trait: they all go up on the way to the turn-around point, and they all go down on the return. That is, they all have their ups and downs. For many of us, the upside is you get all the climbing out of the way first, then you get to rest on the way down. Those of you who suffer from bad knees, or no knees at all, will likely disagree.

Gorge hikes owe their differences to geography; the mountains near the entrance sweep most of the rain from the clouds, leaving the area east of the Cascade crest dry and warm. Sailboard enthusiasts can also be thankful for the geography where the Columbia River gouges a giant funnel for the wind that blows up or down the river.

The trails here are numbered from west to east along that ever-so-convenient yet noisy Interstate 84. Enjoy!

COLUMBIA RIVER GORGE

17. Latourell Falls Loop

RATING	🚶 🚶 🚶
DISTANCE	2.2 miles round-trip
HIKING TIME	1 hour, 30 minutes
ELEVATION GAIN	535 feet
HIGH POINT	650 feet
EFFORT	Moderate Workout
BEST SEASON	Spring
PERMITS/CONTACT	None/Guy W. Talbot State Park, (800) 551-6949
MAPS	USGS Bridal Veil; Green Trails Bridal Veil 428
NOTES	Leashed dogs welcome; good family walk

THE HIKE

Climb a moderately steep trail along a forested hillside to a view of twin-tiered Upper Latourell Falls, returning on the opposite side of the canyon.

GETTING THERE

From Portland, follow Interstate 84 east to exit 28 and follow the exit to the Historic Columbia River Highway 30. Turn right (west) and follow the highway for about 3 miles, passing the Bridal Veil Falls parking area, to the Latourell Falls parking area, 238 feet above sea level. GPS trailhead coordinates: N45°32.333'; W122°13.075'

THE TRAIL

It's difficult to imagine a prettier setting for a waterfall than that of Lower Latourell Falls, right at the parking area. So before you start your climb, walk down the paved trail to the best view of the lower falls, framed by columns of basalt and bright green ferns.

To continue, return to the parking lot to find the Upper Falls trailhead to the east. It begins climbing immediately, first on a steep paved trail that makes the climb easier for tourists to get a look at the lower falls from above. Once the trail reaches an upper viewpoint, the pavement ends and the trail climbs left to a second viewpoint near the top of the falls. From there, it continues through greenery to a steep shortcut trail

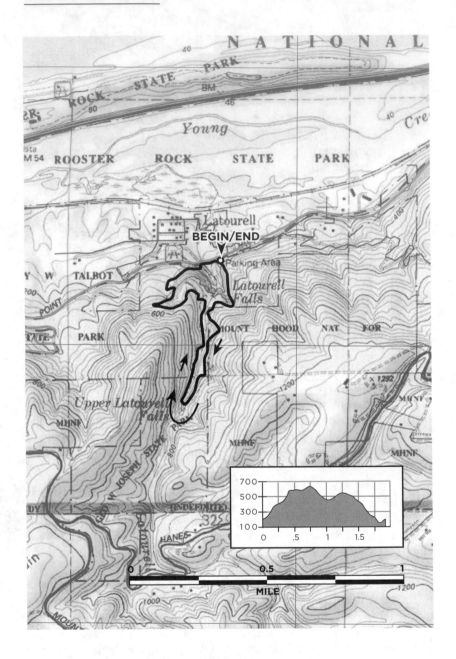

Lower Latourell Falls is the trailhead for the Latourell Falls Loop.

0.3 mile from the trailhead. Stay left here and continue climbing, crossing a couple of tumbling tributaries to Latourell Creek below.

You'll hear the Upper Latourell Falls before you see them, but once you round a final forested corner and descend gently to a bridge crossing, you'll be happy for the energy you spent getting here. You'll see not one but two waterfalls spitting out of moss-decked cliffs at right angles to each other. The trail crosses Latourell Creek just below the lower falls, 0.8 mile from the trailhead, then climbs briefly before beginning a descending traverse through the forest on the opposite side of the creek.

But it's not all downhill from here. At 1.2 miles from the trailhead, you'll find the western junction of the shortcut trail. Stay left and climb a couple of switchbacks to a Columbia Gorge overlook, then drop on a gentle grade along the forested hillside to the west, finally switching back and dropping to the Columbia River Highway 30, about 0.2 mile west of the trailhead. Walk the road back to the parking area across the bridge spanning Latourell Creek.

GOING FARTHER
You can add another 0.3 mile to this hike by crossing the highway and following a trail down to a quiet picnic area, then climbing back up under the Columbia River Highway bridge over Latourell Creek, crossing a footbridge, and passing the viewpoint of the lower falls.

18. Angel's Rest

RATING	🚶 🚶 🚶 🚶 🚶
DISTANCE	4.4 miles round-trip
HIKING TIME	3 hours, 30 minutes
ELEVATION GAIN	1,540 feet
HIGH POINT	1,640 feet
EFFORT	Prepare to Perspire
BEST SEASON	Fall, summer
PERMITS/CONTACT	None/Columbia River Gorge National Scenic Area, (541) 308-1700
MAPS	USGS Bridal Veil; Green Trails Bridal Veil 428
NOTES	Leashed dogs welcome

THE HIKE

This is a tough climb to one of the best vistas in the lower Columbia Gorge.

GETTING THERE

From Portland, follow Interstate 84 east to exit 28 and follow the exit to the Historic Columbia River Highway 30. The parking area for the Angel's Rest Trail No. 415 is on the right, 100 feet above sea level, but I'd recommend the overflow parking lot just west on the Columbia River Highway. From the overflow parking lot, turn uphill to the left, 131 feet above sea level. GPS trailhead coordinates: N45°33.534′; W122°10.453′

THE TRAIL

This hike begins by climbing a forested hillside to the east and crossing an open slope of sharp-edged basalt rocks that won't be comfortable for hikers wearing lightweight tennis shoes. You'll climb around a ridge above Coopey Creek, where you can hear Coopey Falls below before descending gently to a footbridge crossing the creek, **0.7** mile from the trailhead. This is the only water on the hike if you've come armed with a filter bottle, pump, or pills.

Serious climbing begins just beyond the bridge on switchbacks to a viewpoint overlooking the Columbia River Gorge, **1.4** miles from the trailhead. You can also look up to see the bare rocky bluff below Angel's

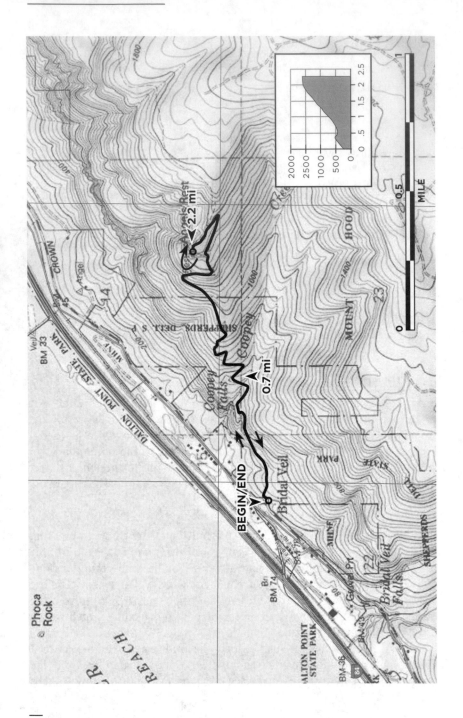

The view upriver from Angel's Rest.

Rest. Continue switching back along a trail that could get mighty slippery in wet weather. In a half-mile, emerge from the forest to a brushy hillside burned by a wildfire about 20 years ago.

The trail continues to climb in switchbacks before turning to the south and crossing a field of flat rocks, finally switching back and climbing to a trail junction at a saddle just below Angel's Rest, to the left. The rocky perch is reached with a short scramble along the crest of the ridge, where the snowy summit of Mount Adams peeks from behind low hills to the northeast.

GOING FARTHER

You can add another mile to your hike by turning right at the junction and climbing 0.1 mile to a junction with the Devil's Rest Trail. Turn left on the Angel's Rest Trail No. 415 and follow it 0.4 mile to a picnic spot and spring in the forest, just east of Angel's Rest.

A longer, much more strenuous option would be to follow the Devil's Rest Trail 1.4 miles and 800 vertical feet up to 2,450-foot high Devil's Rest, making the round-trip hike 7.2 miles.

19. Multnomah Falls

RATING	🚶 🚶 🚶 🚶
DISTANCE	2.4 miles round-trip
HIKING TIME	2 hours
ELEVATION GAIN	750 feet
HIGH POINT	800 feet
EFFORT	Prepare to Perspire
BEST SEASON	Spring; open all year
PERMITS/CONTACT	None/Columbia River Gorge National Scenic Area, (541) 308-1700
MAPS	USGS Multnomah Falls; Green Trails Bridal Veil 428
NOTES	Leashed dogs welcome

THE HIKE

Park and hike from a quiet trailhead, so you can warm up for the short but steep climb to the top of the highest waterfall in the Columbia Gorge.

GETTING THERE

Take Interstate 84 east from Portland to Bridal Veil, exit 28. Exit and drive to the junction with the Historic Columbia River Highway 30 and turn east, or left. Drive 2.5 miles to the Wahkeena Falls trailhead and the Wahkeena Falls parking area, 163 feet above sea level. GPS trailhead coordinates: N45°34.503′; W121°07.650′

THE TRAIL

Multnomah Falls is hugely popular with tourists, and with good reason—at 630 feet from the top of the upper falls to the bottom of the lower cascade, it's one of the tallest in North America. Just up the road from the restaurant, information center, and tourist shop at the giant Multnomah Falls parking lot is a kinder, gentler trailhead at Wahkeena Falls. The 0.6-mile walk along the forested trail leading east from the Wahkeena trailhead will be a good way to limber up for the steep climb ahead.

Follow Trail No. 442 as it climbs briefly above the old Columbia River Highway, then traverses the forested hillside to the east before dropping down to the Multnomah Falls complex. You'll emerge just west of the Multnomah Falls Lodge; walk west to the Multnomah Falls viewpoint,

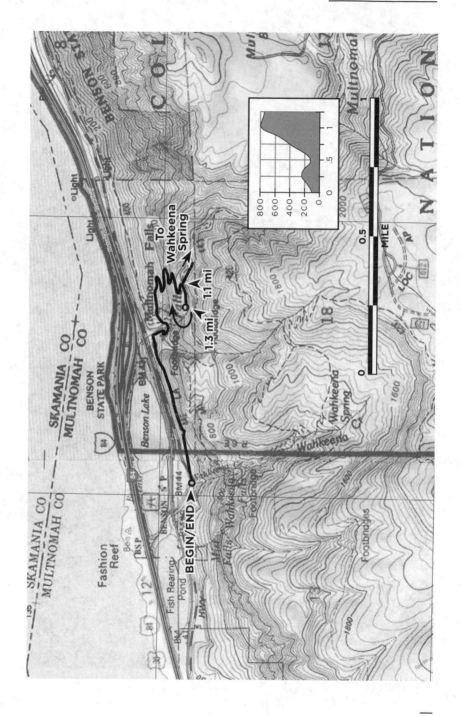

The hike to the top of Multnomah Falls crosses the Benson Bridge, about halfway up.

where a paved trail begins the take-no-prisoners climb up to the Benson Bridge. That's about halfway up the falls.

The paved trail continues climbing in switchbacks, passing a junction with the Columbia Gorge Trail No. 400, where you keep right. It's a half-mile of climbing, gaining nearly 700 feet before topping out in forest above the falls. You'll descend a bit to a trail junction, 1.1 miles from the Wahkeena parking area. Turn right and follow the trail for 0.2 mile to the viewpoint overlooking Multnomah Falls. See all those tiny ant-people down there? After walking down the trail for another 30 knee-punishing minutes, you'll join them.

GOING FARTHER

By continuing upstream from the junction with the viewpoint trail, you can make a strenuous 6-mile loop hike to the Wahkeena parking area. Follow Trail No. 441 to Trail No. 420, turn right and follow Trail No. 420 to Trail No. 419, turn right and take Trail No. 419 to Trail No. 442, then descend on that trail in a steep mile to the parking area.

20. Triple Falls

RATING	🚶 🚶 🚶
DISTANCE	3.0 miles round-trip
HIKING TIME	2 hours
ELEVATION GAIN	550 feet
HIGH POINT	650 feet
EFFORT	Moderate Workout
BEST SEASON	Spring; open all year
PERMITS/CONTACT	None/Columbia River Gorge National Scenic Area, (541) 308-1700
MAPS	USGS Multnomah Falls; Green Trails Bridal Veil 428
NOTES	Leashed dogs welcome; good family hike

THE HIKE

The climb to Triple Falls is a steady ascent through splendid old forest, one of the rare Columbia Gorge walks to leave the sound of Interstate 84 behind.

GETTING THERE

From Portland, follow Interstate 84 east to the Ainsworth exit 35 and follow the signs to the Historic Columbia River Highway 30. Turn west on the highway and drive past Ainsworth State Park to the Oneonta Gorge parking area, just beyond the Oneonta Gorge bridge, 171 feet above sea level. GPS trailhead coordinates: N45°35.328′; W1224.718′

THE TRAIL

The symmetry of three white plumes of water tumbling 85 feet from a forest into a pool is the main attraction for this waterfall hike, a moderately tough climb through a forest of mixed evergreens. Begin by following the Columbia Gorge Trail No. 400 as it climbs west above the old Columbia River Highway for 0.2 mile to a junction with the trail to Triple Falls. Turn left here and continue to climb around the ridge above the Oneonta Gorge to a second junction with a trail that crosses the gorge to Ponytail and Horsetail Falls, about a half-mile from the trailhead.

Stay right here and continue your uphill charge to a switchback, 1.1 miles from the trailhead. Beyond, you'll switchback again and begin a

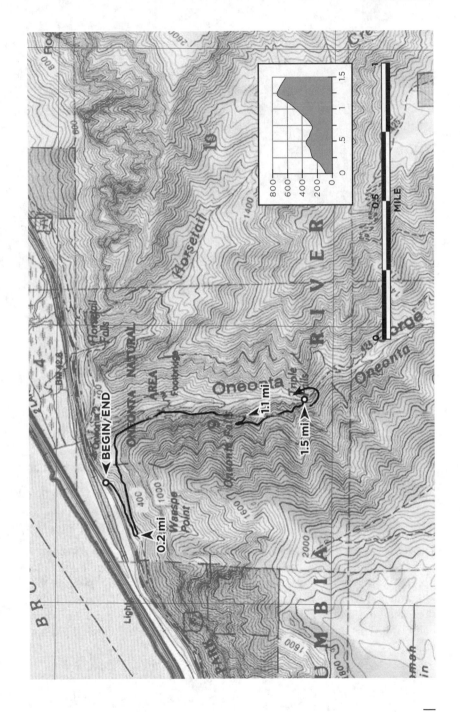

The hike to Triple Falls is a good family walk.

contour to the Triple Falls viewpoint, 1.5 miles from the trailhead. The bridge that once crossed Oneonta Gorge at this point was destroyed and had not been replaced by the summer of 2009.

Many have wondered at the beauty of Triple Falls, which appear to have equal volumes of water pouring over each of the plumes. It is a little-known fact that several years ago, Columbia Gorge National Scenic Area staffers installed computer-controlled pumps to assure continued even flow from each cascade. Feel free to check my research regarding that point.

GOING FARTHER

The best way to extend this hike would be to begin it at the Ainsworth State Park picnic area, 1 mile to the east of the Oneonta Gorge on the old Columbia River Highway. Climb from the picnic area to Gorge Trail No. 400 and follow it west for a mile, passing Horsetail and Ponytail Falls, then climbing and eventually crossing Oneonta Gorge to join the Triple Falls Trail. This option would make the round-trip hike to Triple Falls 4.4 miles.

21. Ponytail Falls

RATING	🚶 🚶 🚶
DISTANCE	2.4 miles round-trip
HIKING TIME	2 hours
ELEVATION GAIN	160 feet
HIGH POINT	260 feet
EFFORT	Easy Walk
BEST SEASON	Spring; open all year
PERMITS/CONTACT	None/Columbia River Gorge National Scenic Area, (541) 308-1700
MAPS	USGS Multnomah Falls; Green Trails Bridal Veil 428
NOTES	Leashed dogs welcome; great family hike

THE HIKE

The youngsters will enjoy this trail because it leads to a waterfall they can walk behind. It's an unusual and interesting perspective.

GETTING THERE

Follow Interstate 84 east from Portland to the Ainsworth exit 35 and turn right at the junction with the Historic Columbia River Highway 30. Follow this highway to the Ainsworth State Park Campground entrance. The trailhead is at the upper campground loop, 124 feet above sea level. GPS trail coordinates: N45o35.733´; W122.03.029´

THE TRAIL

You're never very far from the rush and hustle of the interstate highway on this wooded walk, but once you dip into the canyons of Horsetail and Ponytail falls, you'll swap traffic noise for the much more pleasant sound of tumbling water. Begin by climbing south into the forest for 0.1 mile to a junction with the Columbia Gorge Trail No. 400, which traverses in bits and pieces for almost 40.0 miles along the route of the old highway. Turn right at the junction and continue on the Gorge Trail for 0.5 mile to a junction with a trail climbing from a picnic area below. Stay left, winding along the forested hillside above the old highway.

At **1.1** miles, another trail climbs out of the forest from the Horsetail Falls parking area. Stay left again, and in a few hundred feet, switchback

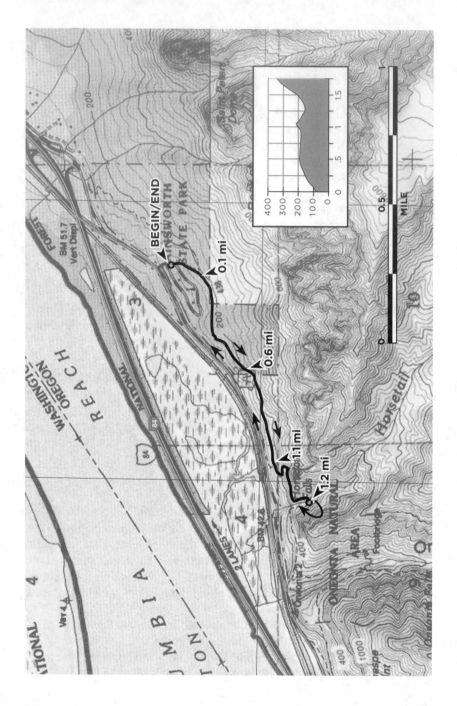

The trail to Ponytail Falls ducks behind the cascade.

to a view of Horsetail Falls before rounding a ridge and dropping into the canyon carved by Horsetail Creek. The trail descends toward Ponytail Falls, then ducks behind the cascade **1.6** miles from the trailhead, where you can watch the water plume splash into a round pool below.

GOING FARTHER
You can continue past Ponytail Falls for another mile to the Oneonta Gorge, cross the gorge, and climb to a junction with the trail to Triple Falls. Turn left at the junction and climb 0.7 mile to the Triple Falls viewpoint. The round-trip hike would thus be 5.4 miles.

22. Gorge Trail 400, Eagle Creek to Bridge of the Gods

RATING	🚶
DISTANCE	4.0 miles round-trip
HIKING TIME	2 hours
ELEVATION GAIN	160 feet
HIGH POINT	240 feet
EFFORT	Easy Walk
BEST SEASON	Winter; open all year
PERMITS/CONTACT	Northwest Forest Pass required/Columbia River Gorge National Scenic Area, (541) 308-1700
MAPS	USGS Bonneville Dam; Green Trails Bonneville Dam 429
NOTES	Bicyclists and leashed dogs welcome; good family hike

THE HIKE

This hike is best left for those drizzly days when all you really want to do is get some exercise and take one of Mother Nature's own showers.

GETTING THERE

Take Interstate 84 about 44 miles east from Portland to the Eagle Creek Recreation Area, exit 41. Turn right at the stop sign and drive to a picnic area and trailhead along Eagle Creek, 120 feet above sea level. GPS trailhead coordinates: N45°63.653′; W121°91.947′

THE TRAIL

A portion of this part of the Columbia Gorge Trail follows the route of the historic highway, and is as popular with bicyclists as hikers. Once around the first hill, sections of it might also be navigable to those who get outside aboard a wheelchair.

Walk north from the parking area to find the wide trail as it passes several buildings on your right. You'll circle east next to the interstate highway for several hundred feet, then turn away from the noise into the forest, where the pathway intersects a trail that drops from the old campground above.

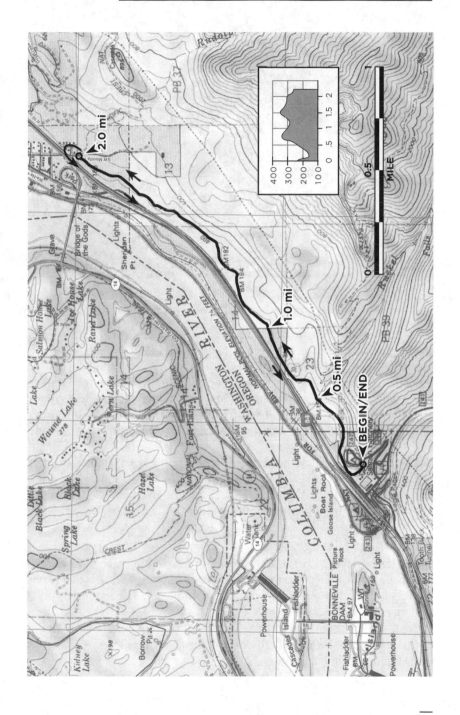

For a longer hike upriver on the Columbia Gorge Trail 400 to Bridge of the Gods, begin at the recently completed Toothrock trailhead.

At **0.5** mile from the trailhead, the Ruckel Creek Trail No. 405 branches to the south and begins its long, steep climb to Hunter's Camp, 5.0 miles upstream. Stay left here and follow the pavement to its end about a mile from the trailhead. This might be a good turnaround point for families with young children. To continue, follow the trail as it alternately climbs and drops through a green forest of alder and maple. At **2.0** miles from the trailhead, you'll strike a gravel extension of Moody Street in Cascade Locks, your turnaround point.

A good picnic spot might be the park at Bridge of the Gods. Turn left and follow Moody Street to the Interstate 84 overpass and look for the trail leading to the park on the left beyond the overpass. It's about 0.2 mile to the park from the turnaround point.

GOING FARTHER

One of the best ways to extend this hike is to start from the new Toothrock trailhead, about a mile west of Eagle Creek. Take the Fish Hatchery exit 40 off Interstate 84 and drive east to the trailhead. The round-trip hike from here would be about 6 miles.

Another significantly more strenuous alternative would be to hike the Ruckel Creek Trail, which climbs steeply for about 5 miles, one-way, out of the Columbia River Gorge.

23. Metlako Falls

RATING	🚶 🚶 🚶 🚶
DISTANCE	4.0 miles round-trip
HIKING TIME	2 hours, 30 minutes
ELEVATION GAIN	400 feet
HIGH POINT	510 feet
EFFORT	Moderate Workout
BEST SEASON	Spring, fall
PERMITS/CONTACT	Northwest Forest Pass required/Columbia River Gorge National Scenic Area, (541) 308-1700
MAPS	USGS Bonneville Dam, USGS Tanner Butte; Green Trails Bonneville Dam 429
NOTES	Leashed dogs welcome

THE HIKE

This is a steady, even climb along the beautiful canyon carved by salmon-rich Eagle Creek to a series of waterfalls, far from the noise of interstate highway traffic.

GETTING THERE

From Portland, follow Interstate 84 east to the Eagle Creek Recreation Area, exit 41. Turn right at the stop sign and drive past a picnic area along a narrow one-lane road above Eagle Creek for 0.2 mile to the trailhead, 160 feet above sea level. GPS trailhead coordinates: N45°45.63.653′; W121°91.947′

THE TRAIL

Choose spring for this hike if you're a waterfall watcher, autumn if you'd rather watch salmon. Either season, this is one of the prime hikes in the Columbia Gorge and one of the very few where you can get away from the roar of the interstate. The Eagle Creek Trail No. 440 begins at stream level and climbs gently and evenly along increasingly steep canyon walls.

At **0.5** mile from the trailhead, the canyon wall grows so steep that many people, including this acrophobe, would call it a cliff. My left hand grew calluses from gripping the cable along the uphill side of the rock

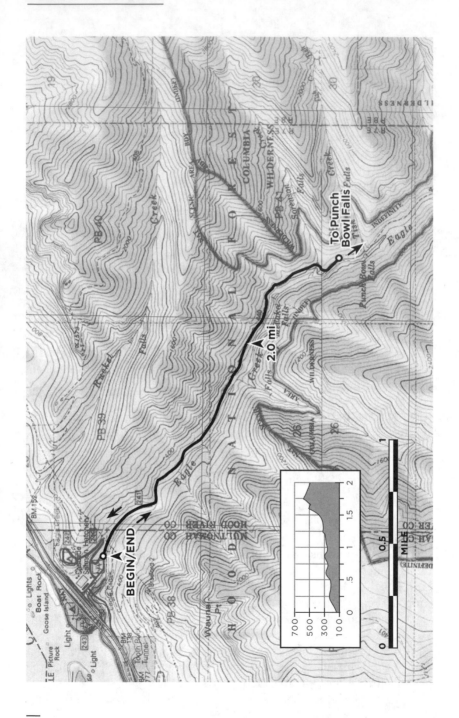

Metlako Falls is among the many waterfalls you'll see while hiking the Eagle Creek Trail.

while walking upstream; my right hand did the same on the return. These rock ledges blasted from the canyon sides are the main reasons this hike isn't recommended for small children, and you'll want to keep a close rein on your kids or grandkids if they're tagging along. The longest section you'll encounter is about 150 yards, though it may seem longer for those of you who, like me, have an irrational fear of heights. ("It's not the height that scares me," one acrophobe once said, "it's the distance I might fall." To which a Real Mountain Climber might reply, "Hey, it's only the last 30 feet or so that kills you.")

The path never strays far from the Eagle Creek canyon, climbing past tributary creeks and over rounded basalt bluffs as the walls of the canyon grow higher above the trail. The trail flattens a bit and enters a hillside forest as it approaches Metlako Falls, the first of several big cascades along the trail, **2.0** miles from the trailhead. A side trail to the right leads steeply down to a viewpoint while a gentler trail descends to the viewpoint about 0.1 mile farther along the main trail.

The Mazamas, a Portland-based hiking and mountaineering club, named the falls in 1915 after the Native American goddess of salmon. You might guess from looking at the falls, about 100 feet high, that not many salmon swim upstream beyond this point. However, white-water kayak zanies have run the falls and lived to show it off on YouTube.

GOING FARTHER

The Eagle Creek Trail No. 440 beckons hikers to continue upstream, with Punch Bowl Falls the next stop, another 0.5 mile, one-way. Loowit Falls is next, with High Bridge about 3 miles from the trailhead. This plank and metal span crosses Eagle Creek about 100 feet above the water. Beyond, the trail drops to Tenas Camp, a good picnic spot 3.4 miles from the trailhead. Perhaps the longest day-hiking option would be Tunnel Falls, where the trail is blasted from rock and you pass behind the cascade. It's 6.2 miles, one-way, to Tunnel Falls.

24. Dry Creek Falls

RATING	🚶 🚶
DISTANCE	4.0 miles round-trip
HIKING TIME	2 hours, 30 minutes
ELEVATION GAIN	680 feet
HIGH POINT	880 feet
EFFORT	Moderate Workout
BEST SEASON	Spring
PERMITS/CONTACT	Northwest Forest Pass required/Columbia River Gorge National Scenic Area, (541) 308-1700
MAPS	USGS Carson; Green Trails Bonneville 429
NOTES	Leashed dogs welcome; good family walk

THE HIKE

The easy grade of this trail makes it a good tune-up for longer and more strenuous walks later in the season. And it's a good hike with children because there's a surprising waterfall at the end.

GETTING THERE

From Portland, take Interstate 84 east to Cascade Locks, exit 44. Drive east 1.5 miles to the town and turn left at the Bridge of the Gods intersection. Follow the road as it loops toward the toll booth and look for a right turn into a rest area and the Bridge of the Gods trailhead for the Pacific Crest Trail No. 2000. The trail is located across the loop road next to the trail sign, 200 feet above sea level. GPS trailhead coordinates: N45°39.754'; W121°53.786'

NOTE: This trailhead is closed in the winter season. A winter trailhead is located off Moody Street, just north of the Interstate 84 overpass. Follow WaNaPa Road east from the Bridge of the Gods intersection for two blocks and turn right on Moody.

THE TRAIL

This is the northern Oregon terminus for the Pacific Crest Trail No. 2000. If you're looking for a slightly longer walk than Dry Creek Falls, you can keep on the Pacific Crest Trail all the way to Mexico. I'm guessing it will take you a bit longer than a day. But after this walk, when somebody

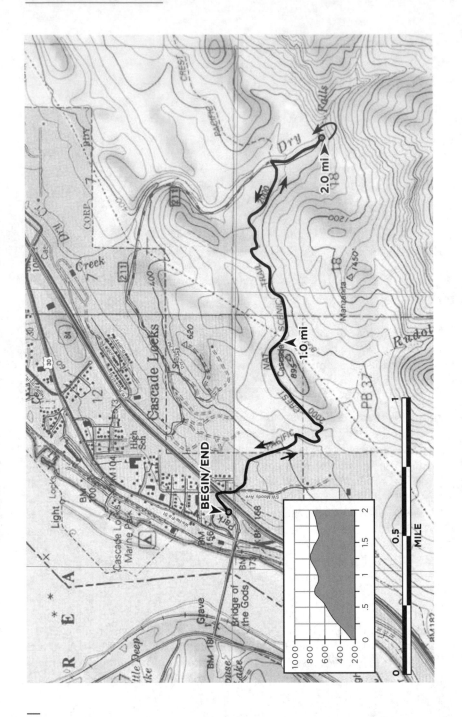

The bridge at Dry Creek Falls is testimony to the fact that Dry Creek isn't always dry.

asks you if you've ever hiked the Pacific Crest Trail, you'll be able to say: "Yes, I have."

The trail parallels the interstate highway for several hundred feet before intersecting a paved road at the Moody Street underpass. Follow Moody Street uphill and bear right on a gravel road for about 100 feet to the winter trailhead. Your route—the Pacific Crest Trail—takes off to the left while the Columbia Gorge Trail 400 (hike #22 in this guide) emerges from the forest on the right.

The trail climbs gently through alder and maple forest past the back-yard of a house before climbing in broad switchbacks to a power transmission line clear-cut, 1.0 mile from the trailhead. Walk around a curve on the power line road, and then find the trail to the right as it re-enters the forest.

At 1.1 miles, you'll cross a forested saddle on a rounded ridge, then begin a gentle descent above a gully. The trail drops gently through the forest and emerges at a gravel road and a bridge crossing Dry Creek. In all but the wettest of times, you should be able to quickly discern why they called it Dry Creek.

The big surprise waits just up the gravel road, which opens to a nice view of the falls. Don't get too close, or you'll find Dry Creek Falls are anything but dry.

GOING FARTHER

As previously noted, you can hike all the way to Mexico on the Pacific Crest Trail. A shorter alternative would be to follow the Pacific Crest Trail for 4.0 miles, one-way, beyond Dry Creek, climbing to Herman Creek Campground. Another alternative for a longer workout would be to start this hike at the Eagle Creek trailhead (hike #23 in this guide). That would make a round-trip walk of 8 miles to Dry Creek.

25. Lancaster Falls

RATING	🚶 🚶
DISTANCE	2.2 miles round-trip
HIKING TIME	1 hour, 30 minutes
ELEVATION GAIN	200 feet
HIGH POINT	350 feet
EFFORT	Easy Walk
BEST SEASON	Spring; open all year
PERMITS/CONTACT	None/Columbia River Gorge National Scenic Area, (541) 308-1700
MAPS	USGS Mount Defiance; Green Trails Hood River 430
NOTES	Leashed dogs welcome

THE HIKE

Easy walking to several waterfalls and a history lesson are the major reasons to take this hike, although if you want some exercise and serious climbing, there's an option for a loop hike.

GETTING THERE

Follow Interstate 84 east from Portland to the rest area at exit 55, 120 feet above sea level. GPS trailhead coordinates: N45°41.304′; W121°41.430′

THE TRAIL

If you aren't in the mood for taking this gentle walk, you might enjoy watching confused hikers trying to figure out which way to go for the various trails leading from the rest area. Most confusing is the blue sign at the entrance to the rest area that reads: "Mount Defiance Trail Access," because it faces the opposite direction as the trail. While I laced up my boots in the summer of 2009 to check this trail, I watched two groups of hikers start up the wrong trail and was able to convince them the sign was actually facing the wrong way.

Indeed, the hike to Lancaster Falls and Mount Defiance begins with a walk past that sign, which you can read upon your return. Pick up the trail by walking west along the rest stop entrance road for about 100 yards before the trail drops into the woods along the interstate. Hike for about 0.3 mile to a junction with the Starvation Creek connector Trail

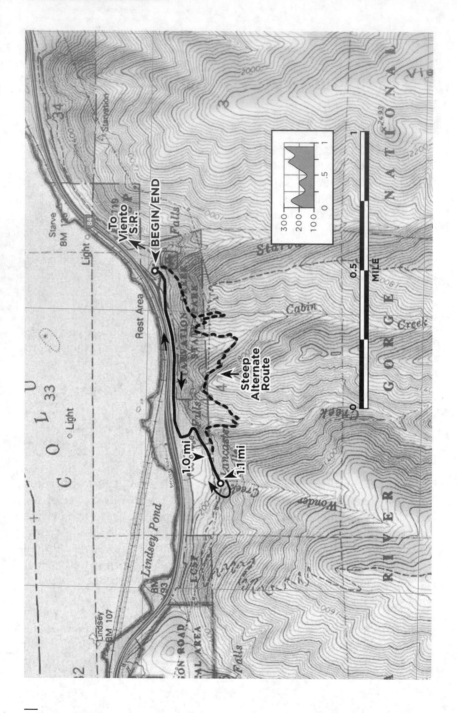

An optional steep, strenuous trail leads to good views of the Columbia River Gorge on the return from Lancaster Falls.

No. 4148 and stay right at the junction. Just beyond, you'll pass a big basalt boulder on the right that hides Cabin Creek Falls, a pretty little cascade that is easy to miss.

Cross Cabin Creek shortly after on a footlog, then hike another quarter mile to the Warren Creek Canyon and cross Warren Creek. You can scramble upstream to Hole-in-the-Wall Falls, named when the creek was diverted through a tunnel to make room for the old Columbia River Highway.

Beyond, the trail begins to climb more steeply as it angles toward Lancaster Falls and Wonder Creek. The path switches back a couple of times, then intersects a trail at **1.0** mile that eventually leads back to the Starvation Creek trailhead. Stay right here and walk another short 0.1 mile to Lancaster Falls. This rather unimpressive cascade was named for Samuel Lancaster, the engineer who designed the anything but unimpressive Historic Columbia River Highway. This is the turnaround point.

GOING FARTHER

Hikers looking for a more strenuous return to the trailhead can turn right at the junction 0.1 mile from Lancaster Falls and begin a long and steep climb up the walls of the Columbia Gorge. This path eventually reaches a stunning and exposed view of the Gorge on a rock outcropping about 800 feet above the river. The trail contours here, then drops into and crosses Cabin Creek before climbing to a junction with the Starvation Creek Trail. Stay left here and begin a very steep descent on the Starvation Creek connector Trail No. 4148 to the Lancaster Falls Trail, 0.3 mile from the trailhead.

Another popular option is the 11-mile round-trip hike to the summit of Mount Defiance, which, despite the sign at the trailhead, is about 4 miles beyond Lancaster Falls.

26. Old Columbia River Highway, Viento State Park

RATING	🚶
DISTANCE	2.4 miles round-trip
HIKING TIME	1 hour, 30 minutes
ELEVATION GAIN	100 feet
HIGH POINT	250 feet
EFFORT	Stroll in the Park
BEST SEASON	Winter; open all year
PERMITS/CONTACT	None/Columbia River Gorge National Scenic Area, (541) 308-1700
MAPS	USGS Mount Defiance; Green Trails Hood River 430
NOTES	Leashed dogs and bicyclists welcome; great family walk; wheelchair accessible

THE HIKE

Walk a section of road that was built back in the age when the scenery along the highway was as important as where the route led, when the destination didn't matter as much as the way you got there.

GETTING THERE

Follow Interstate 84 east from Portland to the Viento State Park exit 56 and follow the signs to the Viento State Park tent campground on the right. The trailhead is located just before entering the campground, 154 feet above sea level. GPS trailhead coordinates: N45°41.758′; W121°56.894′

THE TRAIL

This section of the Historic Columbia River Highway was converted to a trail in 2001, and it serves as a good warm-up to nearby hikes. It also links to the western end of the Lancaster Falls hike (hike #25 in this guide) for a longer trek.

The recently paved trail begins on the southwest end of the parking area and makes a gentle descent along the old highway right-of-way through a forest of maple and alder. Never far from the noise of the interstate highway, the trail meanders through groves of trees before climbing a bit more steeply over a final hill and dropping down to

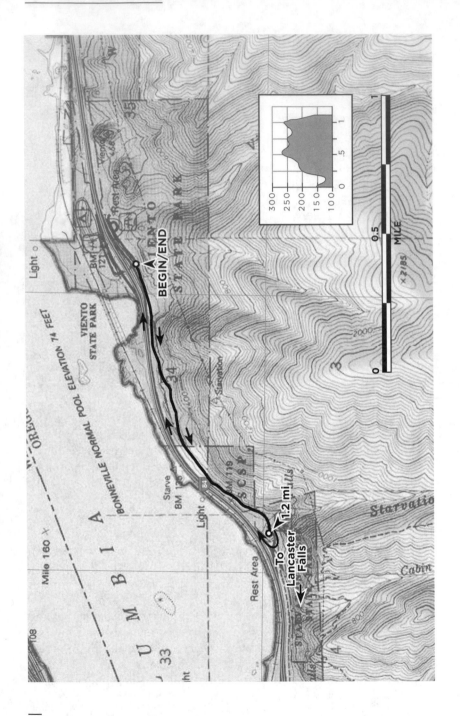

The historic Columbia River trail is wheelchair accessible.

the trailhead at the Starvation Creek rest area. Some folks who get outdoors in wheelchairs will find this hill a bit too steep to navigate without assistance.

GOING FARTHER

The best way to extend this walk is to combine it with the hike to Lancaster Falls, which would make it a round-trip trek of 4.6 miles. For something a bit longer, walk the road down past the Viento State Park auto campground to the boat launch—a great spot for river watching. That adds another 1.6 round-trip miles to your hike.

27. McCall Point

RATING	𝕏 𝕏 𝕏 𝕏
DISTANCE	3.0 miles round-trip
HIKING TIME	2 hours
ELEVATION GAIN	1,000 feet
HIGH POINT	1,722 feet
EFFORT	Moderate Workout
BEST SEASON	Spring
PERMITS/CONTACT	None/The Nature Conservancy of Oregon, (503) 230-1221
MAPS	USGS Lyle
NOTES	Dogs prohibited

THE HIKE
Walk a wildflower-packed trail and climb from a great view of the Columbia River to an even greater view near the sunshine end of the Gorge.

GETTING THERE
Follow Interstate 84 east from Portland to the Mosier exit 69 and turn right to follow the Historic Columbia River Highway 30 through Mosier. Head 6 miles east to the Rowena Crest Viewpoint and trailhead, 700 feet above sea level. GPS trailhead coordinates: N45°040.972′; W121°18.085′

THE TRAIL
You'll have to leave Fido in the car for this walk, as the Nature Conservancy administers the area. You may or may not take this to mean that pets are not a part of the nature that is being conserved by that fine organization. The trail follows an old pioneer wagon route across the plateau for 0.5 mile, where you'll find fields of purple wildflowers in the spring. In this sunny end of the Columbia Gorge, that could be as soon as late March or early April.

Beyond the meadow, the trail begins climbing the lower slopes of McCall Point, named for one of the nation's first "green governors," Tom McCall of Oregon. He served from 1967 to 1975 and was partly responsible for the Oregon "Bottle Bill," environmental cleanup throughout the state, and gaining public ownership of the entire Oregon coastline. You'll

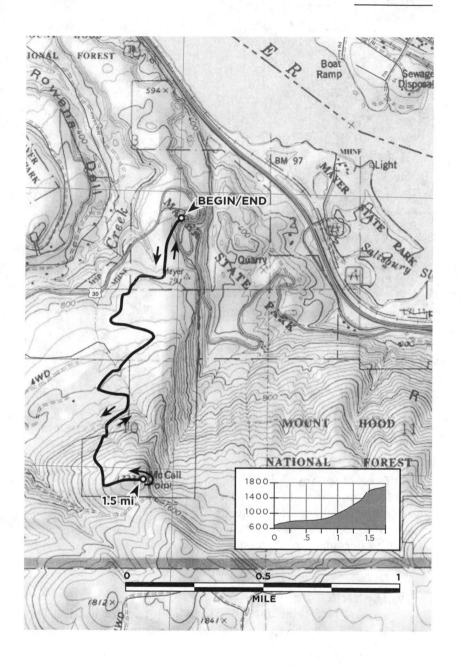

The hike to McCall Point starts at the Rowena overlook on the Columbia River Gorge.

enter a forest of oak trees on the hill, colorful testimony to the fact that you've found your way out of the wet west end of the Columbia Gorge.

The trail gradually steepens toward the summit, with a moderately steep switchback or two toward the end at a picnic turnaround. The vista includes Mount Adams to the northwest and Mount Hood to the southwest.

GOING FARTHER
The best way to extend this hike is to combine it with the Rowena Plateau loop (hike #28 in this guide), making a round-trip walk of 5 miles.

28. Rowena Plateau

RATING	𝕏 𝕏 𝕏
DISTANCE	2.0 miles round-trip
HIKING TIME	1 hour, 30 minutes
ELEVATION GAIN	150 feet
HIGH POINT	700 feet
EFFORT	Stroll in the Park
BEST SEASON	Spring
PERMITS/CONTACT	None/The Nature Conservancy of Oregon, (503) 230-1221
MAPS	USGS Lyle
NOTES	Dogs prohibited; excellent family walk

THE HIKE

Walk a trail through splendid open meadowland carpeted with wildflowers that is also popular with birders in the spring. Cliff-top views of the Columbia River attract photographers throughout the year.

GETTING THERE

Follow Interstate 04 east from Portland to the Mosier exit 69 and turn right to follow the Historic Columbia River Highway 30 through Mosier. Head 6 miles east to the Rowena Crest Viewpoint and trailhead, 700 feet above sea level. GPS trailhead coordinates: N45º040.972'; W121º18.085'

THE TRAIL

Follow the entrance road to the Rowena Viewpoint parking area to the west and cross the road to a trailhead sign marking the beginning of the trail. Climb over the fence on a step and follow the trail across the Tom McCall Preserve. The trail descends very gently to the west, toward basalt cliffs overlooking the Columbia River, and at 0.3 mile you'll strike a trail that heads right and circles the larger of two ponds along the way. Here you'll find a number of wildflowers you may not have encountered in the dry meadow above, along with winged wildlife attracted to the water.

Beyond, the trail continues to the west and the edge of the plateau, where at 1.0 mile, you can look south to the beautiful Rowena Dell and

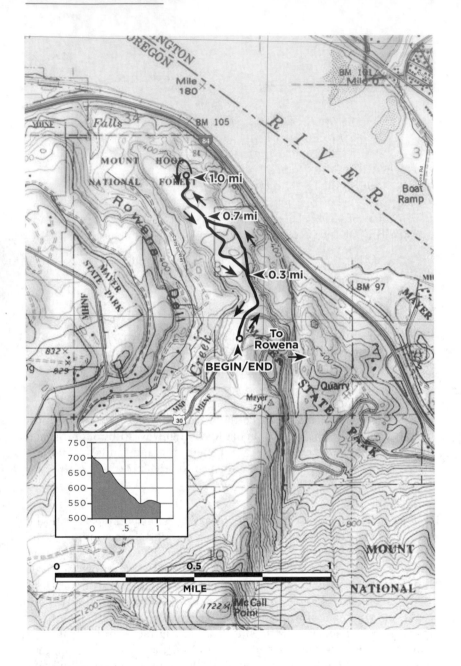

Mount Hood peeks at the balsamroot blooms on the Rowena Plateau hike.

west down the Columbia River to Memaloose Island. To the north is the mouth of the Klickitat River in Washington.

GOING FARTHER
Combine this walk with the trek up to the 1,722-foot summit of McCall Point (hike #27 in this guide) for a round-trip hike of 5 miles.

29. Mosier Tunnels

RATING	🚶 🚶 🚶 🚶
DISTANCE	4.0 miles round-trip
HIKING TIME	2 hours, 30 minutes
ELEVATION GAIN	300 feet
HIGH POINT	580 feet
EFFORT	Moderate Workout
BEST SEASON	Spring, fall
PERMITS/CONTACT	Northwest Forest Pass required/Columbia River Gorge National Scenic Area, (541) 308-1700
MAPS	USGS Lyle
NOTES	Leashed dogs and bicyclists welcome; good family walk; wheelchair accessible

THE HIKE

This section of the old Columbia River Highway has something for everyone: historic tunnels, a view of the river, wonderful sunshine, and a trail surface for bicycles, brave inline skaters, and hikers who take their treks aboard a wheelchair.

GETTING THERE

Follow Interstate 84 east from Hood River to the Mosier exit 69; turn right and follow the old Columbia River Highway to Rock Creek Road and turn left. Follow the signs uphill to the parking area on the left, 272 feet above sea level. A wheelchair access parking area is on the right at the trailhead. GPS trailhead coordinates: N45°40.803´; W121°24.562´

THE TRAIL

It can get mighty hot here in the summer, so I'd suggest the spring or autumn for this walk along the old highway that has been converted for human-powered travel. The paved trail stretches almost 5.0 miles, one-way, from the Mosier trailhead to a visitor center at Hood River, so it is popular with bicyclists.

You'll hike about 2.0 miles, one-way, and start at the Mosier end, which begins with an uphill climb that is likely to be less crowded than the Hood River trailhead. You'll walk uphill for about 0.7 mile, eventually rounding

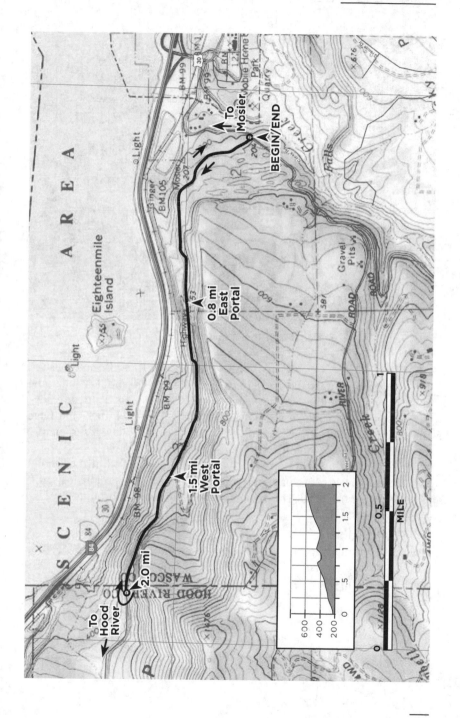

The Mosier Tunnels are one of the attractions along the Historic Columbia River Highway trail.

a bluff and picnic area overlooking the Columbia River. In another 0.1 mile, the route enters the first of two tunnels, each about a half-mile long. They were engineered at a time when scenic vistas were an essential part of auto travel, so portholes were cut in the rock to give drivers and their passengers a view down to the river below. Today, try to picture the view from these windows without the interstate below.

The route continues to drop gently toward the west end of the second tunnel, then levels off to pass one of the original highway mileposts, 2.0 miles from the trailhead. This makes a good spot to turn around.

GOING FARTHER
The trail continues up and down through increasingly greener forest to a Columbia Gorge Visitor Center just east of Hood River, a one-way distance of 4.6 miles.

30. The Dalles Riverfront Trail

RATING	🚶 🚶 🚶
DISTANCE	4.0 miles round-trip
HIKING TIME	2 hours, 30 minutes
ELEVATION GAIN	100 feet
HIGH POINT	200 feet
EFFORT	Moderate Workout
BEST SEASON	Spring, fall
PERMITS/CONTACT	None/Columbia River Gorge National Scenic Area, (541) 308-1700
MAPS	USGS Petersburg
NOTES	Leashed dogs and bicyclists welcome; good family walk; wheelchair accessible

THE HIKE

Walk along one of the newest sections of The Dalles Riverfront Trail, a scenic trek through wetlands home to waterfowl, shoreline-loving birds, and early spring wildflowers.

GETTING THERE

Take The Dalles exit 82 from Interstate 84 and turn left onto Chenoweth Road, which becomes River Road passing under the interstate, and continue about 0.3 mile to River Trail Way. Turn left to a parking area and the trailhead, 105 feet above sea level. GPS trailhead coordinates: N45°37.960′; W121°12.496′

THE TRAIL

Portions of this trail might best be labeled "urban," but after traversing part of an old industrial area, this paved pathway along the riverside and through wetlands being restored by far-thinking members of The Dalles community feels more like a country walk. It's a popular bicycle ride and, except for a steep climb up to the Columbia Gorge Discovery Center, is a wonderful path for those in wheelchairs to get acquainted with Mother Nature.

The path, soon to be a developed trailhead, drops to a bridge crossing wetlands and turns west along the river past Rocky Island, then circles

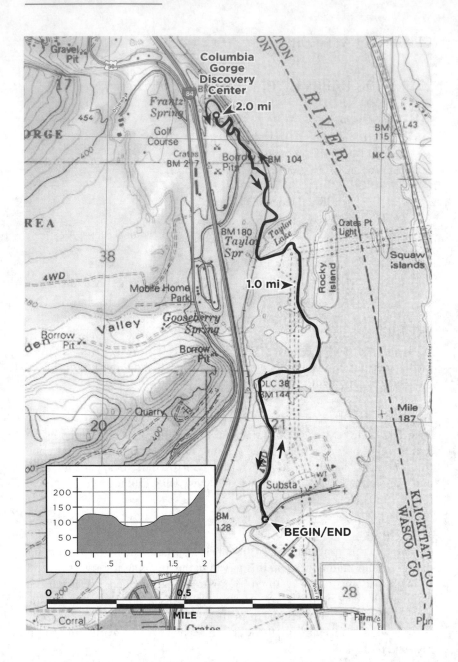

Dog walkers, inline skaters, and bicyclists share the trail with pedestrians on The Dalles Riverfront Trail.

Taylor Lake before returning to the riverside. It meanders through meadows that turn golden in the fall before climbing in switchbacks to the Columbia Gorge Discovery Center. The pond area west of the center is a great spot for a picnic, and the center is the best place to learn all about the history and prehistory of the Columbia Gorge.

Speaking of history, I am compelled to reprint a portion of the heretofore-unknown secret diary of William Clark that I bought from P. T. Barnum IV on eBay. He guaranteed that it was authentic and promised to return my money if I could track him down. In it, Clark—who was camped at Rockfort, near present-day The Dalles—described a dream he had the night of April 18, 1806: "Capt. Lewis and Sgt. Ordway were clad in some shiny cloths that stuck to their bodies. They also wore boots with wheels attached, and rolled along a smooth black trail that reeked of taur. This vision I attribute to the boiled camas roots we ate for supper, which also so filled us of wind that we scarce breathed all night."

I'm willing to part with the diary for half of the $1,439.97 I paid for it.

GOING FARTHER
Though you'll be walking a few of the unfinished sections of The Dalles Riverfront Trail on streets and sidewalks, you can begin your hike almost 3 miles to the east, at The Dalles Riverfront Park. Other trailheads are located along River Road.

31. Deschutes River Trail

RATING	🚶 🚶
DISTANCE	4.0 miles round-trip
HIKING TIME	2 hours, 30 minutes
ELEVATION GAIN	50 feet
HIGH POINT	250 feet
EFFORT	Easy Walk
BEST SEASON	Spring, fall
PERMITS/CONTACT	None/Deschutes River State Recreation Area, (800) 551-6949
MAPS	USGS Wishram, Emerson
NOTES	Leashed dogs welcome; good family walk

THE HIKE

Walk along the banks of the wild Deschutes River, where steelhead—and due to no small consequence—anglers congregate, winged wildlife is plentiful, and Oregon shows another side of its beautiful face.

GETTING THERE

Drive east on Interstate 84 from The Dalles to the Celilo exit 97. Turn right and then left, following signs to the Deschutes River State Recreation Area. The trailhead is at the southernmost parking area, across a grassy field next to the river, 173 feet above sea level. GPS trailhead coordinates: N45°37.781'; W120°54.493'

THE TRAIL

Spring arrives here around the middle of March, which is an excellent time to see wildflowers, but perhaps not the best time to hike this trail. Spring runoff might flood parts of the path, and greening foliage might block views. Autumn could be a better time to walk this trail, which meanders along the river and is used by anglers who by rule must get out of their riverboats to fish from shore.

In the scant 80 miles along the Columbia Gorge, from the green and wet Latourell Falls Trail to the mouth of the Deschutes River, the country-side changes dramatically. The hills and geologic features are more simi-lar, although they are more rounded by erosion at the sunrise end of the

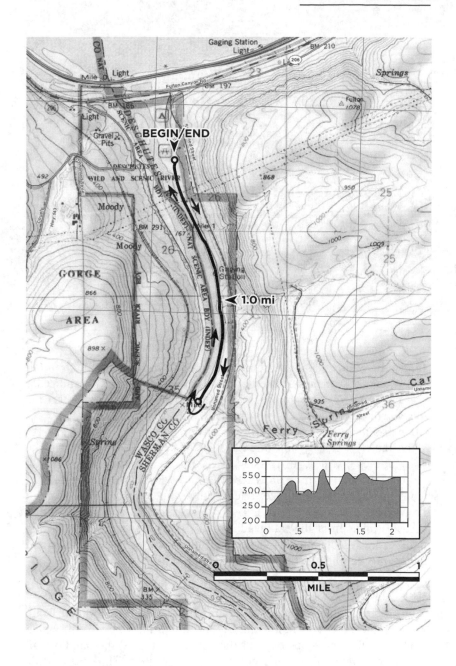

The Deschutes River Trail begins with a walk across the grass of the Deschutes Recreation Area.

Gorge. The weather changes from more than 37 inches of annual rainfall in Portland to 14 inches at The Dalles. Where maple, alder, fir, and cedar trees cover the hills toward the west, sage and golden grasses blanket the hills above the Deschutes.

Benches along the route are provided for hikers who might pause to watch the river roll by and birders who flock to the area to watch the many orioles that nest in riverside trees. The trail follows the riverbank and cuts through high brush where the only view might be the branch about to slap you in the face, released by your hiking partner leading the way.

At **2.0** miles from the trailhead, you'll find a sign and trail pointing uphill to the Middle and Upper Trails. This is your turnaround point and opportunity to find a bench and picnic spot by the river.

GOING FARTHER

From the trail sign at 2 miles, you can climb uphill to the Middle Trail, which is the Deschutes Rail Trail, or beyond to the Upper Trail, which climbs steadily and loops back to the trailhead. Taking the Middle Trail back to the trailhead would yield a round-trip hike of 4.6 miles, while climbing up and down the Upper Trail will give you a strenuous workout of 5 miles.

32. Deschutes Rail Trail

RATING	🚶 🚶 🚶 🚶
DISTANCE	4.0 miles round-trip
HIKING TIME	2 hours, 30 minutes
ELEVATION GAIN	200 feet
HIGH POINT	400 feet
EFFORT	Easy Walk
BEST SEASON	Spring
PERMITS/CONTACT	None/Deschutes River State Recreation Area, (800) 551-6949
MAPS	USGS Wishram, Emerson
NOTES	Leashed dogs and mountain bicycles welcome; good family walk; seasonal opening for equestrians

THE HIKE

The trail follows an old railroad grade that is a good introduction to the sunny end of the Columbia Gorge. It's a fine hike, a good mountain bike ride, and from March through June horses are welcome as well.

GETTING THERE

Drive east on Interstate 84 from The Dalles to the Celilo exit 97. Turn right and then left, following signs to the Deschutes River State Recreation Area. The trailhead is at the entrance to the campground on the east side of the road, 200 feet above sea level. GPS trailhead coordinates: N45°38.059′; W120°54.463′

THE TRAIL

The gentle grade above the wild Deschutes River is suitable to creaky knees of all ages, with the opportunity to hike as far as those knees will carry you. The route extends south for more than 17.0 miles, so wilderness pedestrians with knees and muscles of steel can find their own challenge on this trail. The rest of us can be content with a scenic walk above the river where wildflowers abound in the spring and raptors cruise the thermals high above.

The steepest grade on this walk is the hundred yards you'll climb at the trailhead to reach the abandoned rail bed, where you'll level off and

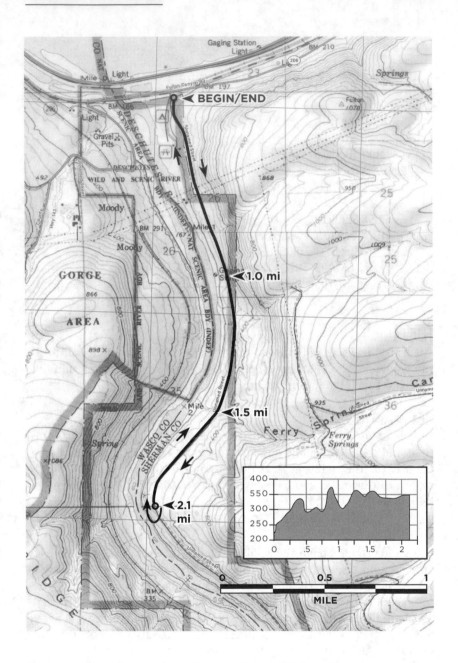

A hiker checks the view from the Deschutes Rail Trail.

walk in sand and gravel. The route contours along hillsides painted by springtime wildflowers, with views to the river below. Look to the skies for the aforementioned raptors and to the ground for the occasional rattlesnake or other reptiles that call these hills home. At 2.0 miles from the trailhead, you'll come to a junction with trails leading to the right to the Deschutes River Trail and to the left to the Upper Trail, which climbs and loops back to the trailhead. Walk a bit farther to the Rattlesnake Rapids viewpoint and look down to see a small bridge sculpted in basalt by Mother Nature.

This makes a good spot to watch the river and enjoy a picnic turn-around.

GOING FARTHER

For a longer walk, follow the trail south as it descends gently to river flats and an old homestead, where you'll see an old rock fence and one of several pit toilets placed along the riverside for anglers and hikers, 3.5 miles from the trailhead. If you'd like an even longer workout, climb back up to the rail trail and hike another 1.1 miles to a seasonal spring just below the trail. That would make a round-trip walk of 9.2 miles.

Rhododendrons provide a showy display in late spring along the Pacific Crest Trail north of Lolo Pass.

MOUNT HOOD

Until a few years ago, I spent all of my hiking time on the south side of Oregon's highest peak, skiing and trekking around Timberline. I am thankful I discovered a much wider area around Wy'East to explore, and I look forward to hiking many more trails I missed the last time around.

The country around the mountain differs from west to east and north to south. Trails around the west side of the peak are wet and forested, while trails to the east and south are dry and support different kinds of forests. In the high country, rhododendrons pop out in the late spring and color the mountains pink. In the fall, berries grow in such profusion it is almost impossible to walk without leaving purple footprints.

Hikes around the mountain are listed here following U.S. Highway 26 south and include two hikes near the south end of Oregon Highway 35, then following Oregon Highway 35 south from Hood River. I hope you'll be as eager to return after taking some of these treks as I am.

MOUNT HOOD

33. Wildwood Recreation Area

RATING	🚶
DISTANCE	3.3 miles round-trip
HIKING TIME	2 hours, 30 minutes
ELEVATION GAIN	65 feet
HIGH POINT	1,230 feet
EFFORT	Easy Walk
BEST SEASON	Spring; open all year (entrance gate open mid-March–Thanksgiving weekend)
PERMITS/CONTACT	Entrance fee required/Bureau of Land Management, (503) 622-3696
MAPS	USGS Rhododendron; Wildwood Recreation Site pamphlet
NOTES	Leashed dogs welcome; excellent family walk

THE HIKE

Here is an excellent walk that offers the chance to learn about wetlands ecology and get a unique view of salmon-spawning territory.

GETTING THERE

Drive 14 miles east on U.S. Highway 26 from Sandy to the Wildwood Recreation Site and turn right at the entrance. If you wish to avoid paying the entrance fee ($5 in 2009), park in the small lot at the left. If you want to continue, pay the day use fee and drive 0.5 mile to the big parking area on the left. The parking area at the entrance is 1,230 feet above sea level. GPS trailhead coordinates: N45°21.346´; W121°59.188´

THE TRAIL

It's easy, in the rush to get to those high mountain views and fresh air, to drive right past the Wildwood Recreation Area, and that would be a big mistake, especially for families with younger children. The trails around the 550-acre site include interpretive trails to wetlands, picnic areas along the tumbling Salmon River, and an underwater viewing window where you might catch a look at juvenile salmon and trout and other underwater critters.

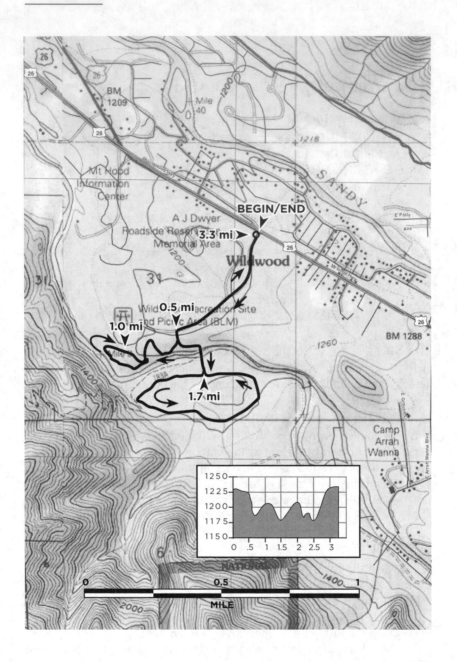

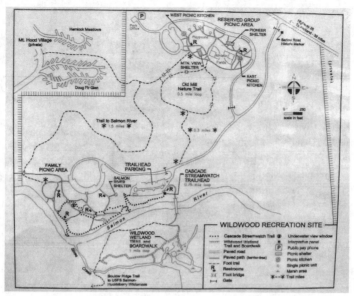

A map at the Wildwood entrance shows the variety of trails available at the complex.

If you've parked outside the entrance gate, hike the main road past the entrance booth for 0.5 mile, turn left, and follow the road into the parking area on the right. Find one of several trails leading out of the parking area to the west, which drop down to follow the banks of the Salmon River and circle uphill 1.0 mile from the trailhead. Follow signs to the underwater viewing window, 0.1 mile beyond. After you've had your fill of fish- or crawdad-watching, continue east to the parking area and turn right to a bridge crossing the Salmon River.

Once across the bridge, turn right at a trail junction 1.7 miles from the trailhead and circle a forested hump that leads to a stream and second trail junction. Turn left here and follow the trail east to a series of boardwalks leading to viewpoints of wetlands, where you're likely to spot anything from herons to frogs. Continue east and circle to the west to the Salmon River bridge; turn right to walk back to the parking area or another 0.5 mile to the Wildwood parking area entrance.

GOING FARTHER

The best way to extend this walk is to hike directly to the Salmon River bridge, turn right, and take the Boulder Ridge Trail No. 783A at the next trail junction to the right, which climbs in 3.8 steep miles to a viewpoint along the ridge.

34. Salmon River Trail

RATING	🚶 🚶
DISTANCE	4.0 miles round-trip
HIKING TIME	2 hours, 30 minutes
ELEVATION GAIN	200 feet
HIGH POINT	1,825 feet
EFFORT	Moderate Workout
BEST SEASON	Spring, summer
PERMITS/CONTACT	Northwest Forest Pass required/Mount Hood National Forest, (503) 622-3191
MAPS	USGS Rhododendron
NOTES	Leashed dogs welcome

THE HIKE

The Salmon River Trail No. 742 is a fine way to tune up after the snow melts in April for longer or more strenuous hikes later in the season.

GETTING THERE

Turn right off U.S. Highway 26 in Zigzag onto the Salmon River Road and follow it 5 miles, keeping left at road junctions, to the big trailhead parking area just before the bridge crossing the Salmon River. The trailhead, 1,700 feet above sea level, is located at the south end of the parking area. GPS trailhead coordinates: N45°16.614′; W121°56.504′

THE TRAIL

Anglers and lots of skinny locals jog this trail to race to fishing holes and stay in shape, and there are several cliffside locations where you might hope you don't encounter a trail speeder. Though angling and physical condition are noble pursuits, they hold some potential for danger, especially if you've got your head down, marveling at some bright yellow stonecrop on the side of the cliff. You might look up only to find the business end of a 7-weight Sage about to poke you in the eye, or a pair of size 11 Nikes bearing down on you. Buck up, hug the uphill side of the trail, and the danger is sure to pass.

The hike begins with a short uphill climb over a minor ridge along the forested hillside, then drops to river level 0.5 mile from the trailhead.

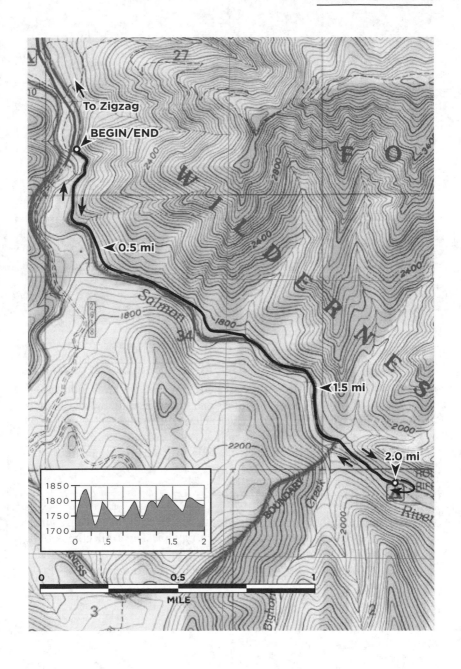

The Salmon River Trail rounds cliffs at river level.

You'll round a rock near the edge of the river, where you should be especially watchful: stonecrop grows here. Beyond, the trail follows the river, climbing in and out of the forest and weaving into and out of side canyons where creeks spill to the river below.

You'll pass a riverside campsite at **1.5** miles from the trailhead, then climb above the river for another 0.5 mile to a second campsite at **2.0** miles, your turnaround point.

GOING FARTHER

To get a more strenuous workout, continue up the trail for as many miles as your knees, lungs, and desire will carry you. The trail climbs at a steady pace, with a few rare steep sections, for 14 miles, one-way. Even joggers and anglers are likely to turn around before that.

35. Pacific Crest Trail North, Lolo Pass

RATING	🚶 🚶
DISTANCE	4.0 miles round-trip
HIKING TIME	2 hours, 30 minutes
ELEVATION GAIN	360 feet
HIGH POINT	3,800 feet
EFFORT	Moderate Workout
BEST SEASON	Summer
PERMITS/CONTACT	Northwest Forest Pass required/Mount Hood National Forest, (503) 622-3191
MAPS	USGS Bull Run Lake; Green Trails Government Camp
NOTES	Leashed dogs welcome

THE HIKE

Bear grass and rhododendrons make the first part of this forested walk a colorful hike along a portion of the Pacific Crest Trail No. 2000.

GETTING THERE

From U.S. Highway 26 in Zigzag, turn north on the East Lolo Pass Road and drive 10.6 miles to the trailhead at Lolo Pass, where the Pacific Crest Trail No. 2000 crosses the road, 3,482 feet above sea level. GPS trailhead coordinates: N45°25.631´; W121°47.332´

THE TRAIL

The views of Mount Hood and surrounding forested valleys make the drive to Lolo Pass worthwhile, even if you never get out of the car. The road is paved all the way to the pass and traverses clear-cut and forest along the way. Of course, you're here for the exercise, so lace up those Vibrams and hit the trail to the north.

The route follows a turnpiked trail for several hundred feet through a wet area, climbs a bit, and enters a clear-cut area underneath electric transmission towers and lines. The buzzing lines must have some positive influence on bear grass and Pacific rhododendrons, because bear grass sprouts everywhere and the slope shouts pink and vanilla from mid-June to mid-July. Climb under the power lines at a gentle grade and enter the forest once again.

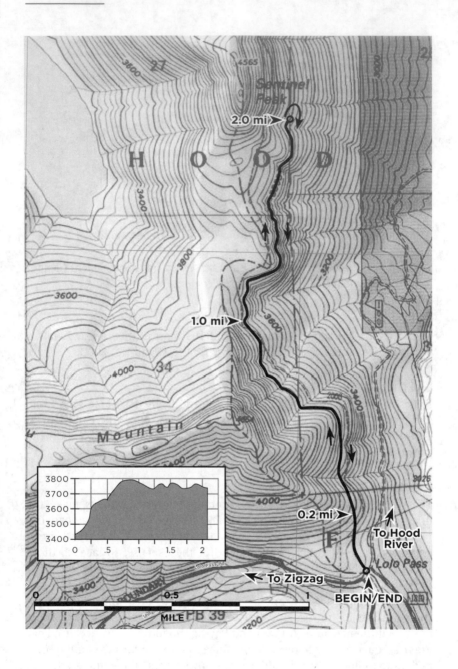

Mount Hood shows off from the Pacific Crest Trail north of Lolo Pass.

Another good time for this outing is later in the summer, when the huckleberries in the forest and thimbleberries in the clear-cut ripen. Once you find a good patch of huckleberries along the trail, however, don't expect to hike too far.

The trail contours underneath a ridge that divides the Hood River drainage from the Bull Run Watershed, which is part of Portland's water supply. The path enters the watershed from time to time, and hikers going that far are asked to stay on the trail. The path passes underneath 4,654-foot Hiyu Mountain, the site of a fire lookout, before

123

continuing its contour through the forest. At 1.0 mile from the trailhead, you'll begin a slight descent toward a broad saddle where the view is hidden by silver fir and hemlock.

Beyond, the trail begins a gentle climb again along the east side of the ridge. It eventually breaks out of the forest to a brushy gully that provides the best view into the Hood River valley below. This is the turn-around point, 2.0 miles from the trailhead.

GOING FARTHER

The path beyond continues along the ridge, contouring to the east around the summit of Sentinel Peak, then descends slightly before crossing a wide saddle and arriving at a junction with a trail that climbs up to the Pacific Crest Trail from Lost Lake. This junction is about 4 miles from the trailhead, yielding a round-trip hike of about 8 miles.

36. Pacific Crest Trail South, Lolo Pass

RATING	🚶 🚶 🚶
DISTANCE	5.4 miles round-trip
HIKING TIME	3 hours
ELEVATION GAIN	960 feet
HIGH POINT	4,375 feet
EFFORT	Prepare to Perspire
BEST SEASON	Summer
PERMITS/CONTACT	Northwest Forest Pass required/Mount Hood National Forest, (503) 622-3191
MAPS	USGS Bull Run Lake; Green Trails Government Camp
NOTES	Leashed dogs welcome

THE HIKE

The view of Mount Hood from the beginning of this hike doesn't get any better, but you'll find plenty of reasons to continue to huckleberry patches in the fall and rhododendron and bear grass gardens in the summer.

GETTING THERE

From U.S. Highway 26 in Zigzag, turn north on the East Lolo Pass Road and drive 10.6 miles to the trailhead at Lolo Pass, where the Pacific Crest Trail No. 2000 crosses the road, 3,482 feet above sea level. GPS trailhead coordinates: N45°25.631′; W121°47.332′

THE TRAIL

The new forest sprouting along the ridge to the south of Lolo Pass will eventually hide the striking view of Mount Hood from the Pacific Crest Trail No. 2000, but for now it should inspire you to burn a few calories. You'll climb directly up the ridge to the south for **0.3** mile, then turn into the forest and begin a climbing traverse for 0.3 mile beyond, reaching a series of a dozen steeper switchbacks through the forest and gaining about 400 feet in 0.5 mile before turning to the west and climbing more gradually to a final switchback, **1.4** miles from the trailhead.

The trail now begins a gentler climb as it contours underneath a 4,534-foot un-named peak and follows the crest of the ridge in the forest for

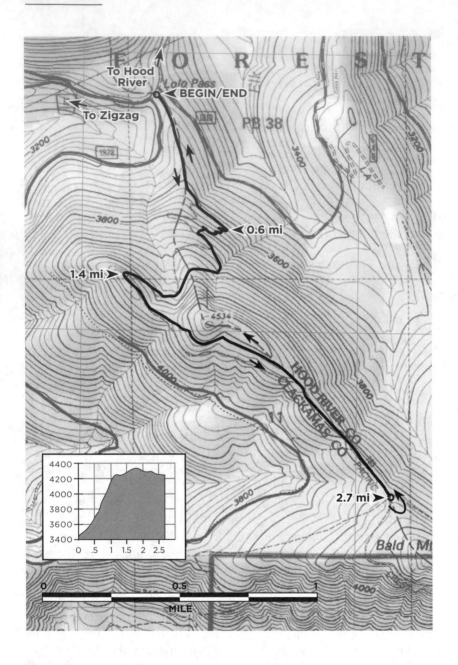

Bear grass and rhododendrons decorate the Pacific Crest Trail south of Lolo Pass.

another 1.3 miles to the site of the Bald Mountain shelter, **2.7** miles from the trailhead. This site marks the junction with the Top Spur and Timberline trails and leads to trails circling Bald Mountain. The forest here prevents anything but peekaboo views.

GOING FARTHER
To extend your hike, you can follow the Timberline Trail around the northeast side of Bald Mountain and return via a new trail that cuts south over the saddle just east of the summit to the Pacific Crest Trail. Turn right on the Pacific Crest Trail to steep meadows and fantastic views on the south slope of Bald Mountain, then continue to the junction with the Top Spur Trail and return the way you came. This short loop would add another 1.2 miles to your hike.

37. Bald Mountain Loop

RATING	🚶 🚶 🚶 🚶
DISTANCE	2.4 miles round-trip
HIKING TIME	2 hours
ELEVATION GAIN	500 feet
HIGH POINT	4,400 feet
EFFORT	Moderate Workout
BEST SEASON	Summer
PERMITS/CONTACT	Northwest Forest Pass required/Mount Hood National Forest, (503) 622-3191
MAPS	USGS Bull Run Lake; Green Trails Government Camp
NOTES	Leashed dogs welcome; good family hike

THE HIKE

Here's a short loop hike that begins with a short, steep climb on the Top Spur Trail No. 785, then rounds a mountain to stunning views of Mount Hood.

GETTING THERE

From U.S. Highway 26 in Zigzag, turn north on the Lolo Pass Road for 4 miles to its junction with Forest Road 1825 and turn right. Follow FR 1825 for 0.6 mile to Forest Road 1828, the follow FR 1828 to the left for 6.5 miles to Forest Road 1828-118 on the right. In summer of 2009, a handwritten sign marked this junction. FR 1828-118 climbs steeply to the right for 1.4 miles to the trailhead, 3,950 feet above sea level. Hikers are asked to park "head-in" at the trailhead. GPS trailhead coordinates: N45°24.434'; W121°47.125'

THE TRAIL

This hike provides a shorter route to the excellent view of the Sandy Glacier and Mount Hood, towering above the Muddy Fork of the Sandy River. It's a no-nonsense climb, popular with hikers who haven't time to take the longer trails from Lolo Pass or Ramona Falls. The trail begins climbing immediately and doesn't let up for the next 0.5 mile, switching back about halfway up the slope.

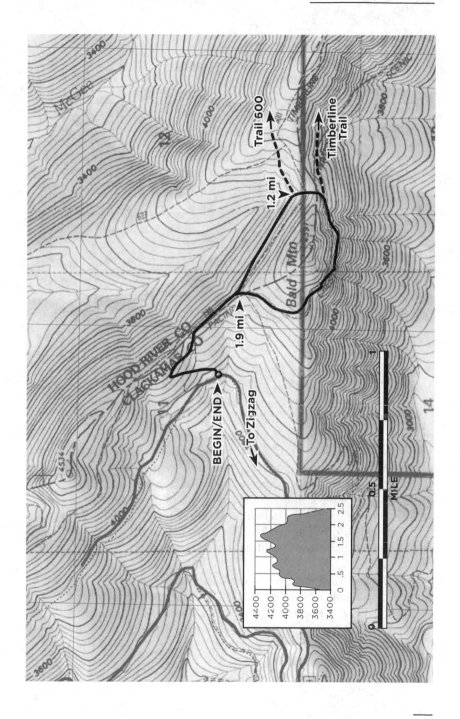

Mount Hood from the Bald Mountain Loop trail.

At **0.5** mile from the trailhead, you'll strike the Pacific Crest Trail No. 2000 as it climbs from Lolo Pass. The trail junction is the site of Bald Mountain Shelter, and the path is kinder and gentler for the remainder of the hike. Follow the Pacific Crest Trail a few hundred feet to a second trail junction with the Timberline Trail No. 600 and follow it to the left. This is a three-way trail junction, with the Pacific Crest Trail dropping steeply to the right. You'll stay left and follow Timberline Trail No. 600 as it traverses along a forested slope on the northeast side of Bald Mountain. You'll pass an unsigned trail junction that climbs to a largely viewless summit of Bald Mountain. Stay left and continue to a second junction with a new connector trail, **1.2** miles from the trailhead, that climbs over a saddle just east of Bald Mountain and drops to the Timberline Trail No. 600.

Turn right at this junction and cross the steep sloping meadows on the south side of Bald Mountain. This is the best spot for views of Mount Hood and the glacier above, less than a mile away. To continue, walk west and circle Bald Mountain to the north, arriving at the three-way junction and shelter site. You've hiked 1.9 miles. Now descend the 0.5-mile trail to the trailhead.

GOING FARTHER

The best way to extend this hike is to follow the Timberline Trail No. 600 to the east after crossing the Bald Mountain saddle. Turn left on the Timberline Trail and hike 2 miles, one-way, as the trail gradually drops about 400 feet to a crossing of the Muddy Fork under the ice of the Sandy Glacier.

38. Mirror Lake

RATING	🚶 🚶 🚶 🚶
DISTANCE	3.0 miles round-trip
HIKING TIME	1 hour, 30 minutes
ELEVATION GAIN	1,400 feet
HIGH POINT	4,900 feet
EFFORT	Moderate Workout
BEST SEASON	Summer, fall
PERMITS/CONTACT	Northwest Forest Pass required/Mount Hood National Forest, (503) 622-3191
MAPS	USGS Government Camp
NOTES	Leashed dogs welcome; good family walk

THE HIKE

Here's a short climb to a lake with a splendid view of 11,239-foot Mount Hood, with an opportunity to climb to even better views beyond.

GETTING THERE

From Zigzag, follow U.S. Highway 26 for 9.2 miles to the big parking area and trailhead on the right, 3,429 feet above sea level. GPS trailhead coordinates: N45°18.408′; W121°47.528′

THE TRAIL

Contrary to the popular notion, Mirror Lake was not so named because it presents a shining reflection of Mount Hood in its still waters. No. I have it on highest authority that Mirror Lake was named for the silent movie actress, Narcissa Mirror, who was among the first women to climb Mount Hood. As you are probably aware, women were summiting many Northwest and Canadian Rocky peaks at the turn of the century. Narcissa later met an untimely end when, while climbing Mount Athabasca in Alberta, Canada, she slipped on a snowfield and—because she was a silent movie actress—was unable to yell for help. Please feel free to check my research on this point.

Begin this hike by crossing Yocum Creek and rounding a forested ridge to the west. The trail climbs continuously at a moderate grade through the forest, swinging back along a broad ridge above Mirror Lake's outlet

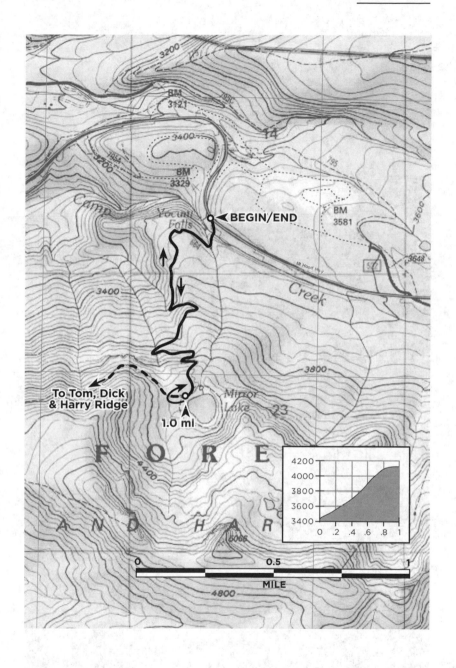

Bear grass grows in profusion along the Mirror Lake trail.

stream. You'll switch back a couple of times along this ridge, emerging at a rocky clearing with a view down the Salmon River valley before dipping into the forest again. The trail approaches the outlet stream at 1.0 mile from the trailhead and turns into the rounded cirque carved by an ancient glacier. Just beyond, the route passes a junction with the trail to Tom, Dick, and Harry Ridge and Mountain. Stay left and round the lake on its west side. The best view of Mount Hood is at the south end of the lake. The trail circles the lake and is 0.5 mile around.

GOING FARTHER
Hikers with stronger knees and larger muscles will probably want to climb farther to better views of Mount Hood and the surrounding Cascades, and the Mirror Lake Trail provides the opportunity. Turn right at the junction and begin the 1.8-mile one-way climb to 5,066-foot-high Tom, Dick, and Harry Mountain. That peak was named for Bill Jones, Ken Korum, and Mickey Soss—a fact I discovered at the same Internet site that outlined the etymology of Mirror Lake.

39. Zigzag Canyon

RATING	🚶 🚶 🚶 🚶
DISTANCE	3.4 miles round-trip
HIKING TIME	2 hours, 30 minutes
ELEVATION GAIN	300 feet
HIGH POINT	6,100 feet
EFFORT	Moderate Workout
BEST SEASON	Summer, fall
PERMITS/CONTACT	None/Mount Hood National Forest, (503) 622-3191
MAPS	USGS Mount Hood South; Green Trail Mount Hood South
NOTES	Leashed dogs welcome; good family hike

THE HIKE

Walk under the shadow of Mount Hood through flower-filled meadows and alpine forests to a look at a big glacier and the canyon carved by water spilling from the ice.

GETTING THERE

Follow U.S. Highway 26 past the Government Camp rest area to the Timberline Lodge Road, turn left, and follow it to the large parking area next to the Timberline day lodge on the left. The trailhead is located uphill and across the road next to the historic Timberline Lodge, 6,000 feet above sea level. GPS trailhead coordinates: N45°19.824′; W121°42.508′

THE TRAIL

The hike east from Timberline Lodge along the Pacific Crest and Timberline trails to the rim of the Zigzag Canyon is one of the easiest high mountain traverses you'll find around Mount Hood. It's difficult to find a part of the hike where there isn't at least a peekaboo view of the big mountain above, and the wildflowers are spectacular throughout the summer. Snowfields linger in shady sections of the trail and you may find patches as late as August.

Several pathways lead to the Timberline and Pacific Crest trails from the parking area, but the most direct is to follow the road toward the historic Timberline Lodge. Climb the paved pathway that rounds the east

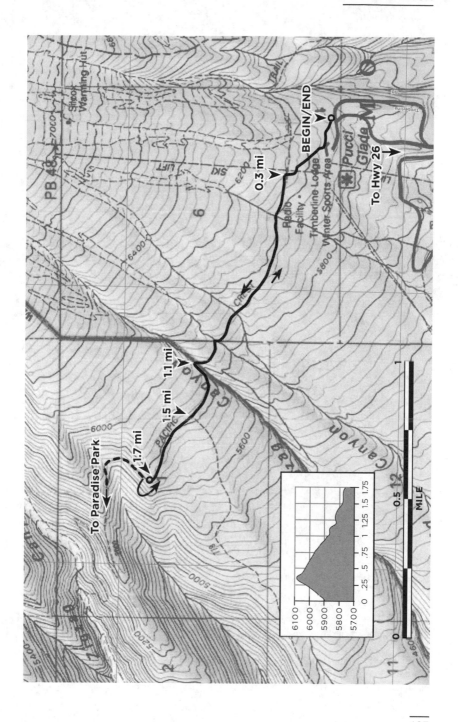

The view of Mount Hood along the Timberline trail to Zigzag Canyon is usually much better than this.

end of the lodge and turns to the west just above on the paved trail. Walk for 0.1 mile west under the Magic Mile chairlift to a junction with the Mountaineer Trail No. 798, which climbs under the chairlifts for 0.3 mile to a junction with the Timberline and Pacific Crest trails. Turn left here and begin a gentle descent in alternating alpine meadows and timberline forest to contour around Sand Canyon and at 1.1 miles, drop into Little Zigzag Canyon.

Cross the boulders in Little Zigzag Creek, which likely won't be too difficult in late summer, and pick up the trail that climbs up the other side. Hike into forest, continuing a gentle descent, to a junction with the Hidden Lake Trail, 1.5 miles from the trailhead. Stay right and continue to drop through the forest to the rim of the Zigzag Canyon, where there's an excellent open viewpoint up the canyon to the receding Zigzag Glacier and rocks above and the canyon below. You're 1.7 miles from the trailhead.

GOING FARTHER
The 1.9-mile trail down to the bottom of the Zigzag Canyon and 1.8-mile Paradise Park Loop is a splendid—if strenuous—hike from the viewpoint. You'll descend at a moderate grade to a junction with the Paradise Park Loop Trail No. 757, then climb into Paradise Park and a junction with a connector Trail No. 778. Turn left and descend in a half-mile to the Pacific Crest Trail. Turn left and descend in 0.4 mile to close the loop and climb back to the viewpoint. The round trip hike to Paradise Park would be about 10 miles.

40. Trillium Lake Loop

RATING	🚶
DISTANCE	1.8 miles round-trip
HIKING TIME	1 hour, 30 minutes
ELEVATION GAIN	Negligible
HIGH POINT	3,620 feet
EFFORT	Stroll in the Park
BEST SEASON	Summer, fall
PERMITS/CONTACT	Day Use Permit required/Mount Hood National Forest, (503) 662-3191
MAPS	USGS Mount Hood South; Green Trails Mount Hood
NOTES	Leashed dogs welcome; excellent family hike

THE HIKE

Circle a subalpine lake with a spectacular view of Mount Hood and walk a plank trail over frog- and flower-filled wetlands.

GETTING THERE

Follow U.S. Highway 26 southeast from Government Camp to the Trillium Lake Road at the Trillium Lake Sno-Park, then turn right and follow the Trillium Lake Road about 3 miles, passing the entrance to the Trillium Lake Campground on the right. Turn right at the entrance to the day use area and trailhead, 3,615 feet above sea level. You can buy a self-issue day use permit ($6 in 2009) at the trailhead. Golden Age and Golden Eagle Passports are *not* accepted. GPS trailhead coordinates: N45°16.028′; W121°44.361′

THE TRAIL

This excellent hike deserves a higher rating, except for the fact that you've got to pay a trail fee to walk here. Still, if you have stumbled across some stimulus money or got a big REI rebate, the trail around Trillium Lake is worth the price. It includes a paved portion for wheelchair access and a solid gravel and plank boardwalk, and it serves up one of the finest views of Mount Hood you can find. With binoculars, you can watch the long lines of Mazamas climbing around the big schrund above Hot Rocks and ski racers training on the Palmer Snowfield.

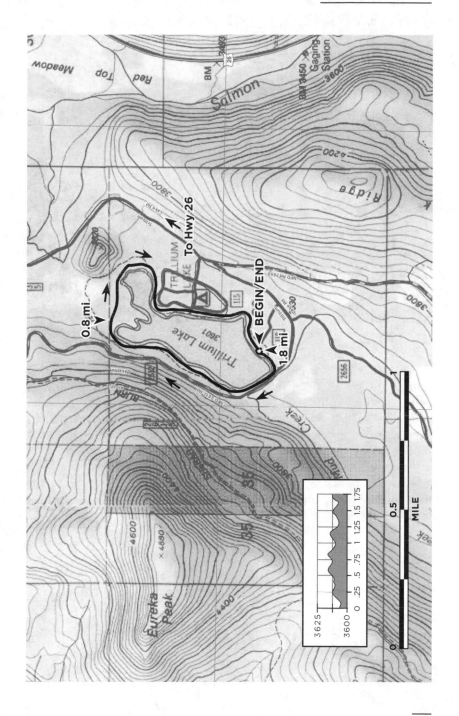

Mount Hood looks down on Trillium Lake.

Begin your walk to the west, or clockwise around the lake. The trail follows the lakeshore in the forest, then emerges near the southwest end of the lake at the Mud Creek dam, where the view across the water of Mount Hood is probably best. The trail rounds the lake and climbs slightly above the shoreline in forest as it heads northeasterly. At **0.8** mile from the trailhead, it turns east and crosses wetlands filled with water-loving wildflowers, including skunk cabbage. Portions of the trail are graveled or plank turnpike. Round the corner of the lake and follow the shoreline of the trail past campground sites to the trailhead parking area, closing the loop at **1.8** miles.

41. Twin Lakes

RATING	🚶 🚶 🚶
DISTANCE	4.2 miles round-trip
HIKING TIME	3 hours
ELEVATION GAIN	550 feet
HIGH POINT	4,400 feet
EFFORT	Moderate Workout
BEST SEASON	Summer, fall
PERMITS/CONTACT	Northwest Forest Pass required/Mount Hood National Forest, (503) 662-3191
MAPS	USGS Mount Hood South; Green Trails Mount Hood
NOTES	Leashed dogs welcome; good family hike

THE HIKE

Climb through forest along a portion of the Pacific Crest Trail No. 2000 to a quiet subalpine lake, with the option of continuing to a second mountain lake.

GETTING THERE

Follow U.S. Highway 26 from Government Camp to the Frog Lake Sno-Park at Wapinitia Pass and find the trailhead at the northern end of the big parking lot, 3,925 feet above sea level. GPS trailhead coordinates: N45°13.744'; W121°41.932'

THE TRAIL

On a hot summer afternoon, this is an excellent hike that offers a chance to cool off in the mighty cold water of Twin Lake at your turnaround point. The trail can get crowded on weekends, but weekday walking can actually be lonely.

The trail wanders north for a few hundred feet to a junction with the Pacific Crest Trail No. 2000, where you'll turn right and begin a gentle climb through the subalpine forest as the trail gets gradually steeper. Climb about a half-mile before switching back and continuing to climb past a small spring for another half-mile. The trail flattens as it gains a forested saddle and, at 1.4 miles from the trailhead, arrives at a junction with the Twin Lakes Trail. Turn right and climb gently over the crest of

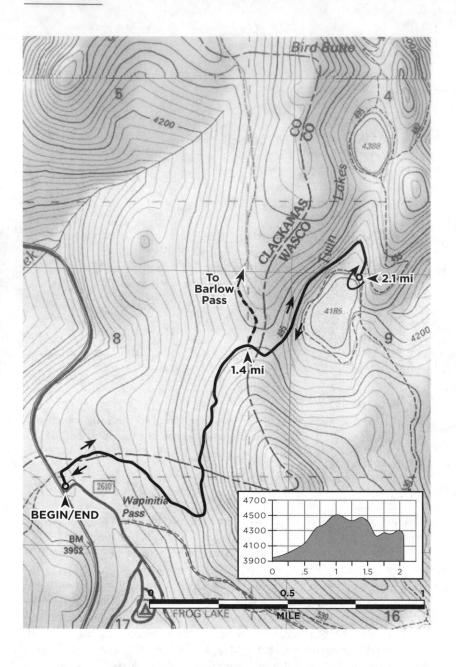

Human and canine hikers enjoy the Twin Lakes trail.

the saddle and begin a traversing descent to the north through the forest. The trail traverses the hillside above the first Twin Lake, then turns and switches back to a trail junction just above the lake. Turn right and descend to the lakeshore, your turnaround point **2.1** miles from the trailhead. A trail circles the lake.

GOING FARTHER

For a longer hike, continue past the trail to the lakeshore as it climbs 0.7 mile to the second Twin Lake, which is 200 feet higher than the first. You can circle the lake on a 0.2-mile trail to the east or a 0.4-mile trail to the west, then climb around Bird Butte to the north to a connector Trail No. 495. Turn left and follow that trail back to Pacific Crest Trail No. 2000, 1.2 miles from the upper Twin Lake. Turn left on the Pacific Crest Trail and walk 1.4 miles to the Twin Lakes Trail Junction, then return the way you came. The total distance would be 6.9 miles.

42. Barlow Road

RATING	🥾
DISTANCE	4.8 miles round-trip
HIKING TIME	3 hours
ELEVATION GAIN	700 feet
HIGH POINT	4,172 feet
EFFORT	Moderate Workout
BEST SEASON	Fall
PERMITS/CONTACT	Northwest Forest Pass required/Mount Hood National Forest, (503) 622-3191
MAPS	USGS Mount Hood South; Green Trails Government Camp
NOTES	Leashed dogs welcome; bikes and autos on sections of trail

THE HIKE

This gentle downhill walk through old forest follows a portion of the historic wagon road that brought Oregon settlers over Barlow Pass.

GETTING THERE

Follow U.S. Highway 26 south from Government Camp to its junction with Oregon Highway 35, then take Highway 35 east to Barlow Pass and turn right at the Barlow Pass Sno-Park to the trailhead, 4,172 feet above sea level. GPS trailhead coordinates: N45°16.957′; W121°41.121′

THE TRAIL

Though much of the old wagon road is overgrown and difficult to traverse, a portion of it follows the existing forest road along Barlow Creek for miles downstream. Take a look at the Barlow Road interpretive sign at the trailhead before walking down the road toward the historic Barlow Guard Station. Though the road is used by mountain bicyclists and autos, it is usually quiet and lonely during the week.

The route was hewn from the forest in 1846 by Sam Barlow and Philip Foster and served as the last segment of the Oregon Trail. It began in the area now called The Dalles and follows the White River to Barlow Pass and beyond, more than 100 miles.

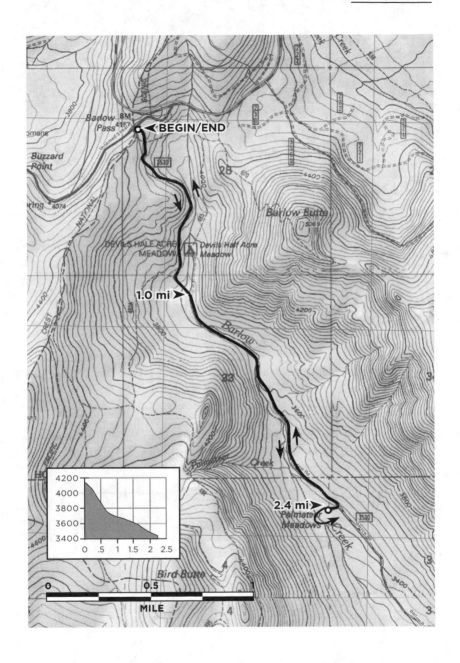

A sign at the beginning of the Barlow Pass trailhead explains the history of the Barlow Road.

You'll pass a junction with the Devil's Half Acre Trail No. 482a, staying left, and in another 0.1 mile, cross Barlow Creek to a junction with a road leading to the Devil's Half Acre Meadow and campground, 1.0 mile from the trailhead. Stay right at the junction and continue walking down the road above the creek in deep forest to Palmateer Meadows and Grindstone Campground, 2.4 miles from the trailhead. This is your turnaround point.

GOING FARTHER

You can descend another 2 miles, one-way, by following the Barlow Road to Klingers Camp. That would total a round-trip hike of 8.8 miles.

43. Palmateer Loop

RATING	🚶 🚶
DISTANCE	5.5 miles round-trip
HIKING TIME	3 hours, 30 minutes
ELEVATION GAIN	450 feet
HIGH POINT	4,575 feet
EFFORT	Moderate Workout
BEST SEASON	Fall
PERMITS/CONTACT	Northwest Forest Pass required/Mount Hood National Forest, (503) 622-3191
MAPS	USGS Mount Hood South; Green Trails Government Camp
NOTES	Leashed dogs welcome

THE HIKE

Hike along the Pacific Crest Trail No. 2000 through old forest along a ridge, then loop back to a view of Barlow Ridge and Mount Hood before returning to the Pacific Crest Trail.

GETTING THERE

Follow U.S. Highway 26 south from Government Camp to its junction with Oregon Highway 35, then take Highway 35 east to Barlow Pass. Turn right at the Barlow Pass Sno-Park to the trailhead, 4,172 feet above sea level. GPS trailhead coordinates: N45°16.957′; W121°41.121′

THE TRAIL

You'll get good views from only two points along this trail, so a cool autumn day when it is cloudy or foggy might be a better time for this walk. The evergreens along much of the route are huge and draped by green mosses that seem to wave and whisper among themselves when the wind blows gently.

The hike begins with a climb along a forested ridge crest west of the trailhead along the Pacific Crest Trail No. 2000, gaining most of the elevation in the first 1.0 mile. There, it joins with the Palmateer Trail No. 482, your path on the return. Stay left at this junction and continue on the Pacific Crest Trail for another 1.1 miles to a junction with the Twin

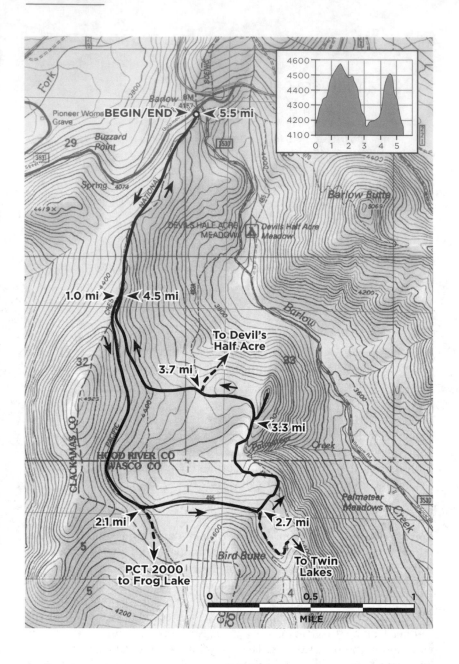

Portions of the Palmateer Loop hike follow the Pacific Crest Trail, which is closed to bicyclists

Lakes Trail No. 495. Leave the Pacific Crest Trail to the left and follow the Twin Lakes Trail for 0.6 mile to a southern junction with the Palmateer Trail No. 482, **2.7** miles from the trailhead.

Turn left at this junction and follow the Palmateer Trail as it contours around Palmateer Creek, passing a viewpoint and side trail leading to a knob overlooking Barlow Creek at **3.3** miles. Stay to the left at this junction and walk another 0.4 mile to a junction with the Devil's Half Acre Trail, **3.7** miles from the trailhead. Stay left and continue another 0.8 mile to the Pacific Crest Trail junction, and walk north to the trailhead.

GOING FARTHER

A longer, more strenuous loop hike continues on the Pacific Crest Trail for 1.4 miles beyond the Palmateer Trail to the Twin Lakes Trail, then turns and drops to Twin Lakes, returning to the Pacific Crest Trail after another 2.7 miles. This loop would make a hike of 8.3 miles.

44. Timothy Lake West

RATING	🚶 🚶 🚶 🚶
DISTANCE	4.2 miles round-trip
HIKING TIME	2 hours, 30 minutes
ELEVATION GAIN	30 feet
HIGH POINT	3,300 feet
EFFORT	Moderate Workout
BEST SEASON	Summer, fall
PERMITS/CONTACT	Northwest Forest Pass required/Mount Hood National Forest, (503) 662-3191
MAPS	USGS Timothy Lake, Wolf Peak; Green Trails High Rock
NOTES	Leashed dogs welcome; great family walk

THE HIKE

This walk around the south shore of Timothy Lake passes several camp-grounds, crosses a small inlet stream, and provides a splendid view of Mount Hood.

GETTING THERE

Follow U.S. Highway 26 from Government Camp to the Skyline Road (Forest Road 42) and turn right. Take Skyline Road 9 miles to a junction with Forest Road 57 and turn right. Drive 1 mile on FR 57 to the Oak Fork Campground on the right and follow the signs to the day use area, 3,264 feet above sea level. GPS trailhead coordinates: N45°06.960′; W121°46.291′

THE TRAIL

Begin by hiking west along Timothy Lake Trail No. 529, which hugs the shoreline for about 0.2 mile before passing in front of the Gone Creek Campground. The route makes a broad turn around a point and heads into a wide bay to a junction at a seasonal creek crossing, **0.9 mile** from the trailhead. Your route is to the right, on Timothy Lake Trail No. 528, but this junction and the creek might make a good turnaround point for families with young children. They can make a loop hike by follow-ing Trail No. 528 to the left, which in 1.0 mile intersects the road to the

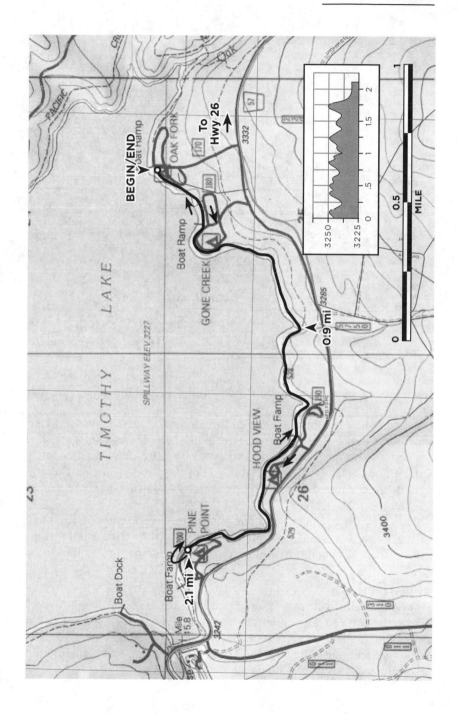

The hike west along the Timothy Lake shoreline passes several campgrounds with good views of Mount Hood.

Gone Creek Campground. Follow it downhill to the shore, turn right, and return to the trailhead.

Beyond the junction the trail continues to the west, never straying far from the shoreline, to the western loop of Hoodview Campground. I am certain you are astute and have ascertained by now that Hoodview Campground is the best place on this side of the lake to pause and admire Mount Hood across the water. The boat ramp and beach here are among the nicest on the reservoir.

Walk past the campground along the shore, then round a narrow bay to the south, following the trail north again to the Pine Point Campground. This is a good turnaround spot, **2.1** miles from the trailhead.

GOING FARTHER
From Pine Point, you can follow Timothy Lake Trail No. 528 1.5 miles across the outlet and around the west end of the lake to Meditation Point, and another 2.9 miles to the inlet stream. Turn right on the Pacific Crest Trail and follow it south for 3.4 miles to the Oak Fork Campground and trailhead. This would total a 12.5-mile loop hike.

45. Timothy Lake North

RATING	🚶 🚶 🚶
DISTANCE	4.2 miles round-trip
HIKING TIME	2 hours, 30 minutes
ELEVATION GAIN	120 feet
HIGH POINT	3,360 feet
EFFORT	Moderate Workout
BEST SEASON	Summer, fall
PERMITS/CONTACT	Northwest Forest Pass required/Mount Hood National Forest, (503) 662-3191
MAPS	USGS Timothy Lake, Wolf Peak; Green Trails High Rock
NOTES	Leashed dogs welcome; good family walk

THE HIKE

Here's a nice, easy portion of the Pacific Crest Trail that follows the shores of Timothy Lake and connects to trails that circle the lake, passing a number of excellent lakeshore campgrounds.

GETTING THERE

Follow U.S. Highway 26 from Government Camp to the Skyline Road (Forest Road 42) and turn right. Take Skyline Road 9 miles to a junction with Forest Road 57 and turn right. Drive 1 mile on FR 57 to the Oak Fork Campground on the right and follow the signs to the day use area, 3,264 feet above sea level. GPS trailhead coordinates: N45°06.960'; W121°46.291'

THE TRAIL

The trail around Timothy Lake serves up some great views of Mount Hood, quiet shoreline forests, and easy terrain for wildlife viewing and walking. The 12.5-mile loop around the lake is popular with mountain bikers, but most of this hike is along the Pacific Crest Trail No. 2000, where bicycles are prohibited.

The trail to the east and north begins by circling past the boat launch and rounding the point to the east along the lakeshore. At **0.4** mile from the trailhead, you'll cross the Oak Grove Fork of the Clackamas River to a junction with the Pacific Crest Trail, where mountain bikes

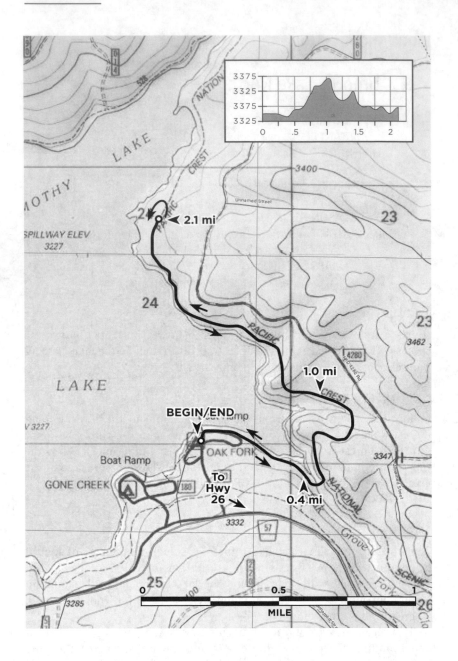

Kayakers paddle on Timothy Lake offshore from the Timothy Lake trail east from Oak Creek Campground.

are prohibited. Turn left and follow the Pacific Crest Trail as it climbs briefly around a forested bluff above the lake and arrive at the summit of a rounded peninsula where you can look through trees to the western shore of the lake, **1.0** mile from the trailhead.

Continue as the trail drops back to the shoreline and follow the shore-line for a short distance, rounding a wide bay and arriving at your turn-around point, just above a small peninsula. This little point, **2.1** miles from the trailhead and just below the trail, might make a good spot for a picnic.

GOING FARTHER

You can continue another 1 mile along the Pacific Crest Trail to the nar-row northeast end of Timothy Lake, where you can cross the inlet and follow the Timothy Lake Trail No. 528 around the north side of the lake. The northern lakeshore trail leads southwest for 2.9 miles to Meditation Point Campground and beyond, 1.5 miles to the southwest end of the lake. To complete the loop, you'd hike 3.3 miles east to the campground.

46. Lost Lake Loop

RATING	🚶 🚶
DISTANCE	3.0 miles round-trip
HIKING TIME	1 hour, 30 minutes
ELEVATION GAIN	Negligible
HIGH POINT	3,180 feet
EFFORT	Easy Walk
BEST SEASON	Fall
PERMITS/CONTACT	Day use permit required/Mount Hood National Forest, (541) 352-6002
MAPS	USGS Bull Run Lake; Green Trails Government Camp
NOTES	Leashed dogs OK; great family hike

THE HIKE

This easy loop is extremely popular, with its fine view of Mount Hood across the lake and the campground and resort along the shore of the lake.

GETTING THERE

Take Hood River exit 62 from Interstate 84 and drive east to 13th Street. Turn right and follow 13th uphill through the Hood River Heights business district and merge with Tucker Road. Follow Tucker around two 90-degree corners to a left-hand turn at Windmaster Corner. Follow Tucker Road 8 miles to the Dee intersection, turn right past the old Dee mill, then turn left onto Lost Lake Road. Follow it 13.7 miles to Lost Lake, where you'll be asked to pay a $7 (in summer 2009) day use permit. Follow the road to the trailhead at the north parking lot, 3,182 feet above sea level. GPS trailhead coordinates: 45°29.788′; W121°49.345′

THE TRAIL

If you're cheap like me (although I prefer the term "thrifty"), you'll park just above the Lost Lake entrance booth and save yourself the day use fee, adding an extra mile, round-trip, to your hike. In any case, walk or drive to the trailhead and begin by walking southwest in forest along the lakeshore. You'll find a number of side trails leading to the shore of the lake and the best views of Mount Hood across the water. A clearing has

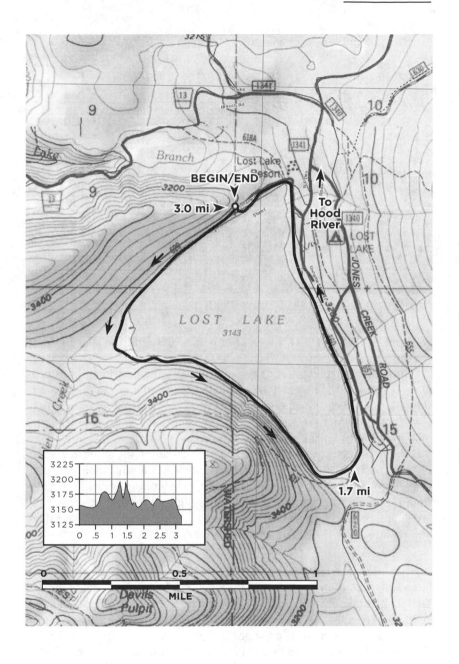

The view of Mount Hood is the attraction for the Lost Lake Loop.

been cut in the trees and a memorial bench makes a fine spot to enjoy the scene.

Fall is the best time to take this walk because the crowds of both people and mosquitoes are likely to be smaller. The pathway stays above the shoreline in forest, with peekaboo views of Mount Hood, then drops to a wetland and inlet creek crossing at the southwest end of the lake, **0.8** mile from the trailhead.

Here the trail turns to the southeast and climbs a bit along the shore in forest, rounding a ridge from Huckleberry Mountain, then dropping slightly to a junction with the Huckleberry Mountain Trail, **1.7** miles from the trailhead. Just past the junction, the trail turns north along the lakeshore, passes the Lost Lake Resort and Campground, crosses a bridge at the outlet, and closes the loop at **3.0** miles.

GOING FARTHER

For a longer and more strenuous hike, follow the Huckleberry Mountain Trail as it climbs for 2 miles to a junction with the Pacific Crest Trail No. 2000. Don't expect to hike the entire distance if the berries for which this mountain was named are ripe. The round-trip hike from the Pacific Crest Trail junction would be **7** miles. To add another 2 miles round-trip, turn right on the Pacific Crest Trail and continue climbing to a saddle between Preacher's Peak and Devil's Pulpit.

47. Tamanawas Falls

RATING	𝕜 𝕜 𝕜
DISTANCE	3.0 miles round-trip
HIKING TIME	2 hours
ELEVATION GAIN	480 feet
HIGH POINT	3,440 feet
EFFORT	Moderate Workout
BEST SEASON	Fall
PERMITS/CONTACT	Northwest Forest Pass required/Mount Hood National Forest, (541) 352-6002
MAPS	USGS Dog River; Green Trails Mount Hood
NOTES	Leashed dogs welcome; good family walk

THE HIKE

The hike to Tamanawas Falls is a nice alternative to the steeper waterfall hikes in the Columbia Gorge, with an opportunity to climb to a niche in the rock behind the falls.

GETTING THERE

From Oregon Highway 35 in Hood River, drive south for about 24 miles to a wide parking area at the highway curve just north of Sherwood Campground. Look for the trailhead sign near the middle of the parking area, 3,040 feet above sea level. GPS trailhead coordinates: N45°23.328′; W121°34.290′

THE TRAIL

The fortunate among you who are retired can take this hike on an autumn weekday, when the trail could well be yours, and yours alone. Local residents enjoy this hike in the summer, when things get hot and dry in the Gorge and they can find shady, cool relief along the trail to the falls.

A new bridge crosses the East Fork of Hood River and joins with the Hood River Trail No. 650. Turn right and follow that trail as it gently drops through an evergreen forest, then climbs to a steep slide area overlooking the highway and river. The trail turns and descends to a footbridge across Cold Spring Creek, then joins with Trail No. 650a, **0.7**

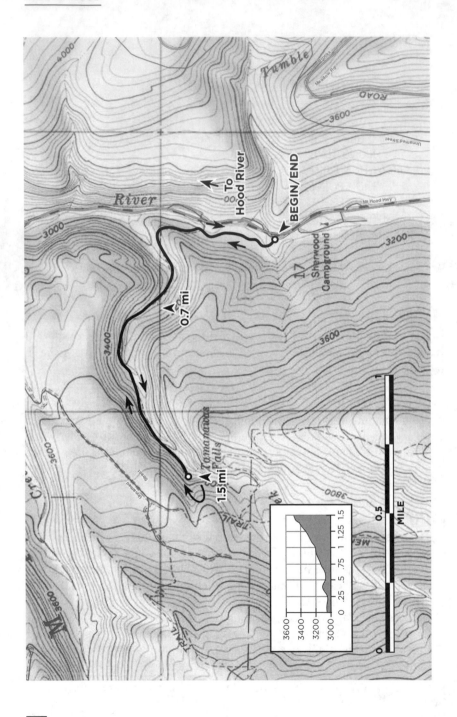

A footbridge crosses the Hood River on the trail to Tamanawas Falls.

mile from the trailhead. Turn left at the junction and follow the creek upstream as it cascades over mossy rocks below the trail.

The route continues to climb a bit steeper and passes a junction with Trail No. 650b. Stay left here and continue another 0.3 mile to the end of the trail at a viewpoint overlooking the falls, 1.5 miles from the trailhead. You can scramble across rocks to the falls, where you can climb to the niche behind the falls.

GOING FARTHER

To add mileage to your hike, you can return to the junction with Trail No. 650b and climb to the left for 0.3 mile to a junction with Elk Meadows Trail No. 645. Turn left and climb 0.8 mile to a second junction with the Lamberson Spur Trail No. 644. From here, you can climb right on the Lamberson Spur Trail to its end in 2.6 miles, or left along the Bluegrass Ridge Trail, which climbs more than 5 miles along Bluegrass Ridge or Elk Meadows.

48. Tilly Jane Loop

RATING	🏃 🏃 🏃 🏃 🏃
DISTANCE	2.6 miles round-trip
HIKING TIME	3 hours
ELEVATION GAIN	900 feet
HIGH POINT	6,600 feet
EFFORT	Prepare to Perspire
BEST SEASON	Summer
PERMITS/CONTACT	Northwest Forest Pass required/Mount Hood National Forest, (541) 352-6002
MAPS	USGS Mount Hood North; Green Trails Mount Hood
NOTES	Leashed dogs welcome

THE HIKE

This hike is a strenuous climb—both up and down—with terrific views of Mount Hood and of the Hood River country below, as well as of the snow giants across the Columbia River.

GETTING THERE

From Oregon Highway 35 in Hood River, drive south for about 22 miles to Forest Road 3510. Turn left and follow it about 2.5 miles to the Cooper Spur Inn and Forest Road 3512. Turn left on FR 3512, the Cooper Spur/Tilly Jane Road, and follow it 9.5 rough miles to the Cloud Cap-Tilly Jane Campground junction. Turn right to the Cloud Cap trailhead, 5,800 feet above sea level. GPS trailhead coordinates: N45°24.141´; W121°39.295´

THE TRAIL

OK, let's get the history out of the way right now, before we run out of breath climbing Cooper Spur Trail No. 600: "Tilly Jane" was what the friends of Mrs. William Ladd called her. That was waaay back in 1889 (even before I was born), when she and her husband bought the Mount Hood Trail and Wagon Road Co. They renamed it the Mount Hood Stage Co. and began improving the road to Cloud Cap immediately. From the feel of it, no improvements have been made since.

Though this hike begins in deep forest, you'll break out above timberline in less than a half-mile and enjoy most of the hike with views in

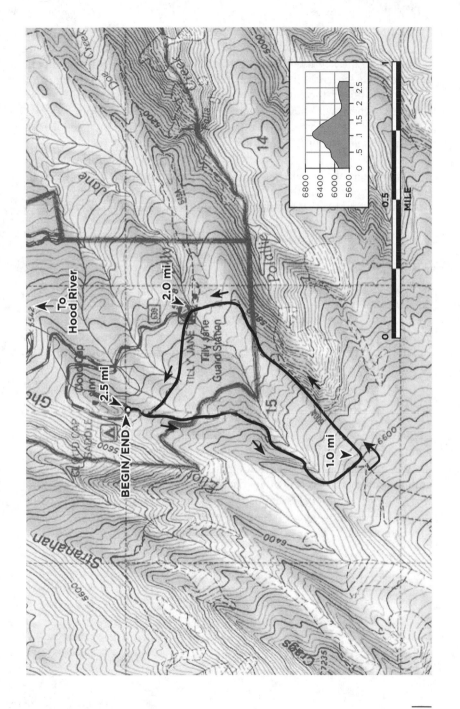

every direction. Begin by climbing past a junction with Trail No. 600a on the left, a few hundred feet above the trailhead. This is your return trail.

Stay right and begin climbing through forest decorated with an understory of huckleberries. The trail soon turns to soft volcanic sand and basalt rock above the infant Tilly Jane Creek. It continues to climb at a moderate pace with several short, steep sections and contours toward the creek. You'll emerge from the forest and climb along the creek before crossing it and climbing to a three-way junction, 6,600 feet above sea level and 1.0 mile from the trailhead. This is a great spot for a rest and a look around: above is Mount Hood and the Eliot Glacier; to the south, the barren volcanic slopes of the mountain. Gaze to the north, to the Hood and Columbia river valleys, with Mount Adams and, on a clear day, Mount Rainier beyond.

You'll turn left from the junction and begin dropping on the Tilly Jane Trail No. 600a, which begins a steep, no-nonsense descent toward the Tilly Jane Campground. This trail follows the edge of the Polallie Creek Canyon and soon drops into open forest 1.5 miles from the trailhead. At 2.0 miles, you'll arrive at a junction with the Polallie Ridge Trail No. 643a, where you'll turn left and cross Tilly Jane Creek, staying above the Tilly Jane Campground on Tilly Jane Creek Trail No. 600a, which traverses west through the forest for 0.4 mile to close the loop. Turn right to the trailhead.

GOING FARTHER

The most scenic and strenuous way to extend this hike is to follow the Cooper Spur Trail No. 600b as it climbs from the three-way junction for about 2 miles up Cooper Spur past a climber's hut along an increasingly steep moraine that splits the Eliot and Newton Clark glaciers. The trail climbs almost 1,800 vertical feet from the junction to a point on the ridge where mountaineers begin their climb up the steep North Face of Mount Hood, and where you should save whatever is left of your knees for the descent.

The north side of Mount Hood overlooks the Tilly Jane Loop hike.

Light shines through the old forest along the South Breitenbush trail.

CENTRAL OREGON

It's always easy to spot someone on Interstate 5 who is heading to Central Oregon to play outside. It would take at least six Yakima racks to tote all the toys. There's a white-water kayak on the roof next to a pair of skis or a snowboard, a backpack crammed in the back window, 165 feet of 11mm flapping from the trunk, mountain bikes dangling from the rack, two 7-weight Sages waving in the wind, perhaps even a set of golf clubs and . . . OMG! Where are little Missy, Junior, and Fido?

Few outdoor playlands in all of America can compare to the number and quality of types of fun you can have in Bend and Sisters, Redmond, and yes, even Les Schwab country. Thank goodness all we have to worry about here is hiking; that's a big enough burden as it is. Trails in this guide are listed from south to north along Forest Road 46, and west to east along Oregon Highway 22 and U.S. Highway 26. I've included several along the Cascade Lakes Highway and U.S. Highway 97. Prineville will just have to settle for last place. I hope Jim and Anna Pettis won't mind.

CENTRAL OREGON

49. Dark Lake

RATING	🚶 🚶 🚶
DISTANCE	4.2 miles round-trip
HIKING TIME	2 hours
ELEVATION GAIN	200 feet
HIGH POINT	4,670 feet
EFFORT	Moderate Workout
BEST SEASON	Summer, fall
PERMITS/CONTACT	None/Mount Hood National Forest, (503) 630-6861
MAPS	USGS Olallie Butte; Green Trails Breitenbush
NOTES	Leashed dogs welcome; great family hike

THE HIKE

This walk along the shoreline of one of Oregon's larger high lakes serves up great views and a trek to a more remote lake beyond.

GETTING THERE

From Oregon Highway 22 in Detroit, turn left onto Forest Road 46, an excellent paved road. Follow FR 46 for 2.9 miles to Forest Road 4690. Turn east on FR 4690, following the signs to Olallie Lake (in summer of 2009, this sign was painted with an arrow on the road), and drive 8 miles to Forest Road 4220. Turn right on FR 4220, drive 5.1 miles to an intersection with Forest Road 4220-170, and turn left to a picnic area and trailhead, 4,977 feet above sea level. GPS trailhead coordinates: N44°48.860′; W121°47.390′

THE TRAIL

Olallie Lake—and the many smaller lakes in this splendid alpine setting—is certainly one of the most beautiful mountain spots in the entire Northwest. The lakes are scattered on a vast plateau overlooked by Mount Jefferson to the south and 7,215-foot Olallie Butte to the east. Trails of varying lengths strike out through Olallie Scenic Area in all directions, and one of the easiest follows the shore of the big lake to the southeast.

To begin, walk the road to the Paul Dennis Campground to the official trailhead at the southeastern end of the campground, 0.4 mile from the parking area. Continue on the trail along the lakeshore, taking in the

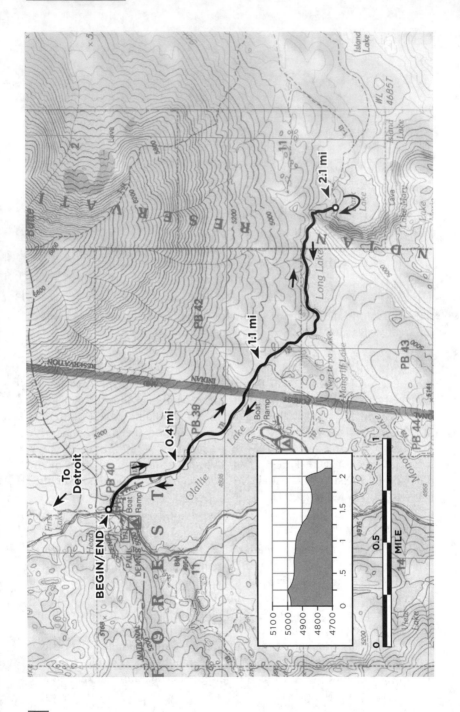

Mount Jefferson rises above a tarn on the hike to Dark Lake.

view of the lake and Mount Jefferson to the south. You'll walk to the end of the lake, 1.1 miles from the parking area, to a trail junction with the Olallie Lake shoreline trail. Stay left and drop in 0.2 mile to the western shore of Long Lake and follow it to the east, climbing down a steep hillside to tiny Dark Lake, with its lava cliffs circling the lake to the west. This is your turnaround point and a good spot for a picnic.

GOING FARTHER

A long and steep loop hike of more than 7 miles heads from the east end of Dark Lake and climbs northeast to a junction with a trail climbing to the summit of Olallie Butte. From there, the trail drops in steep switchbacks to a junction with the Pacific Crest Trail No. 2000 and a trail heading south to Olallie Lake.

50. South Breitenbush Gorge

RATING	🧍 🧍 🧍
DISTANCE	4.4 miles round-trip
HIKING TIME	2 hours, 30 minutes
ELEVATION GAIN	300 feet
HIGH POINT	2,800 feet
EFFORT	Easy Walk
BEST SEASON	Spring
PERMITS/CONTACT	Northwest Forest Pass required/Willamette National Forest, (503) 854-3366
MAPS	USGS Breitenbush Hot Springs
NOTES	Leashed dogs welcome; great family hike

THE HIKE

This is a walk through an impressive old forest that follows a tumbling river below, pink with rhododendrons in the spring and teeming with huckleberries in the fall.

GETTING THERE

From Oregon Highway 22 in Detroit, drive northeast on Forest Road 46 for 11 miles to Forest Road 4685 and turn right. Follow FR 4685 for 1 mile to a wide turn in the gravel road and the signed trailhead on the right, 2,633 feet above sea level. GPS trailhead coordinates: N44°46.517′; W121°57.252′

THE TRAIL

I missed both the rhododendron show in May and the huckleberry feast in August by taking this hike in July. Don't make that mistake. Despite my lack of timing, I still enjoyed this hike through a beautiful old evergreen forest of Douglas fir, hemlock, and cedar. The gorge carved by the South Breitenbush is splendid and it is little wonder the trail was awarded the rare honor of being named a National Recreation Trail.

Perhaps the only advantage of taking this walk when the "only" reward is the scenery is that you're not likely to have company on the trail, especially on a weekday. Hikers are headed to higher vistas in the summer. Begin by walking a few hundred yards from the trailhead over the

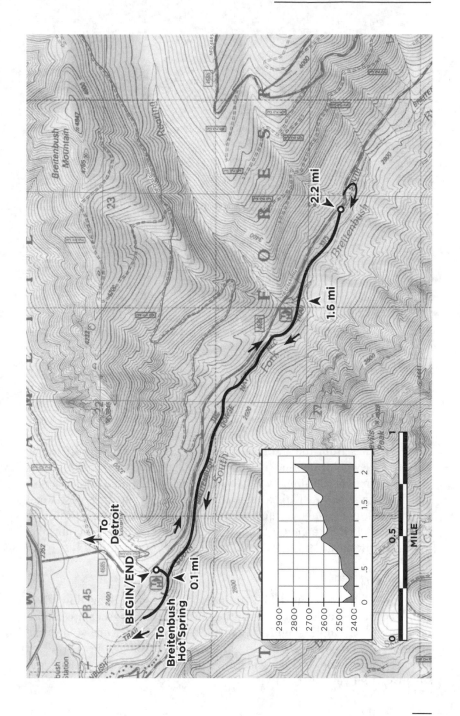

Rhododendrons are thick along the trail above the South Breitenbush Gorge.

crest of a round ridge to find a junction with the National Recreation Trail. The way right leads in 1.0 mile to Breitenbush Hot Springs; you'll want to turn left and begin meandering through the forest. The trail alternately rises and falls in gentle sections, as if the forest itself were drawing sleepy breaths.

At **1.5** miles from the trailhead, you'll find a trail leading off to the right to a viewpoint overlooking the Breitenbush Gorge. Wooden planks in this section can be slippery in wet weather. Just beyond, at **1.6** miles, you'll find a junction with a trail climbing steeply up to Forest Road 4685, which climbs above the trail for several miles. Continue through the forest and begin a gentle climb to the turnaround point of your hike, the eastern trailhead at FR 4685, **2.2** miles from your trailhead.

GOING FARTHER

On your return, you can add 2 round-trip miles by hiking downriver from the trailhead junction to Breitenbush Hot Springs campground, then returning. Another option is to pick up the trail from your turn-around point and follow it upstream. The trail follows the gorge for another 4 miles, and you can walk until the ibuprofen bottle tempts you, sirenlike, from your first-aid kit.

51. Crown Lake

RATING	🚶 🚶 🚶
DISTANCE	3.2 miles round-trip
HIKING TIME	2 hours
ELEVATION GAIN	360 feet
HIGH POINT	4,850 feet
EFFORT	Easy Walk
BEST SEASON	Summer, fall
PERMITS/CONTACT	Northwest Forest Pass required; self-issue Wilderness Permit required/Willamette National Forest, (503) 854-3366
MAPS	USGS Breitenbush Hot Springs
NOTES	Leashed dogs welcome; good family hike

THE HIKE

Climb along a forested ridge, then descend to several alpine lakes with views above the trees of Mount Jefferson to the south.

GETTING THERE

From Oregon Highway 22 in Detroit, drive northeast on Forest Road 46 for 11 miles to Forest Road 4685 and turn right. Follow Forest Road 4685 for 8.4 miles to its end and the trailhead, 4,670 feet above sea level. GPS trailhead coordinates: N44°46.147′; W121°53.647′

THE TRAIL

I made the mistake of following directions to the trailhead that began with the words "Drive about 7.0 miles," so I drove "about" 7.0 miles and found a choice of two bumpy, rutted logging roads, one of which allegedly led to the trailhead. I picked the most likely road and nursed my little front-wheel-drive Honda along the ruts, cleaning the oil pan nicely on the weeds and rocks sprouting from the hump between the ruts. Sure enough, after 0.9 mile, I arrived at the end of the road and a trailhead sign pointing to Crown Lake.

But as it turns out, there are a couple of trails leading to this bright little gem in an alpine basin on the edge of the Mount Jefferson Wilderness. Though shorter, the trail I chose is not the best trail to the lakes,

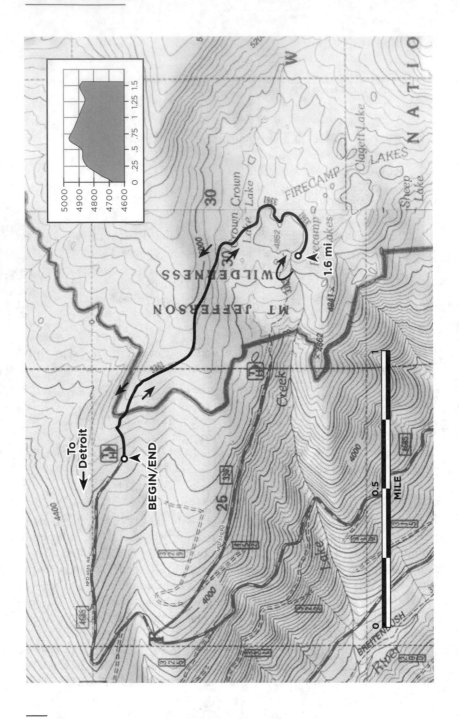

A sign marks one of the trails leading to Crown Lake.

collectively known as the Firecamp Lakes. So, when you arrive at a junction "about" 7.0 miles along Forest Road 4685, follow the well-graded road as it climbs around a curve to the east and circles west around a minor drainage. The road then switches back to the east around a sharp ridge and ends at a nicer trailhead, 8.4 miles from the junction of FR 46 and FR 4685.

After you've issued yourself a Wilderness Permit, begin by climbing a sharp forested ridge through an old clear-cut to the southeast on a moderate grade that climbs 360 feet in 0.7 mile, where the ridge flattens a bit and enters old forest. You'll contour through the forest to the south, then begin a gentle descent to Crown Lake. The trail circles the east end of the lake to a junction with the shorter trail that descends to the alternate trailhead, 1.6 miles from your trailhead. This is a good place to turn around and return the way you came.

GOING FARTHER

The Firecamp Lakes basin is a great place for exploration, with two other named lakes and several tarns in the forest around Crown Lake. To reach Clagett Lake, head southeast from Crown Lake for 0.2 mile. Sheep Lake lies 300 yards beyond, to the southeast. From there, you can climb about 100 feet and turn to the north for 0.2 mile to find a third lake above Clagett Lake, then continue 0.3 mile northwest back to Crown Lake. This circumnavigation of the basin would total 4 miles round-trip.

52. Triangulation Peak

RATING	𝗑 𝗑 𝗑 𝗑
DISTANCE	4.2 miles round-trip
HIKING TIME	2 hours, 30 minutes
ELEVATION GAIN	640 feet
HIGH POINT	5,434 feet
EFFORT	Moderate Workout
BEST SEASON	Summer, fall
PERMITS/CONTACT	Northwest Forest Pass required/Willamette National Forest, (503) 854-3366
MAPS	USGS Mount Bruno
NOTES	Leashed dogs welcome

THE HIKE

This climb through the forest leads to a spectacular view of Mount Jefferson and a chance to explore a cave down a steep, rocky slope below Triangulation Peak.

GETTING THERE

Follow Oregon Highway 22 southeast from Detroit for 6 miles and turn left onto McCoy Creek Road (Forest Road 2233). Drive 7.8 miles to a road junction and keep right. Drive 1.3 miles to a junction with Forest Road 635, then turn right on FR 635 to the trailhead parking area on the right, 4,788 feet above sea level. GPS trailhead coordinates: N44°43.289′; W121°56.09′

THE TRAIL

The surprise of this hike is the view you'll get from the rocky summit of Triangulation Peak, which is difficult to distinguish from the forest ridges looking to the east from the trailhead. The peak is the site of an old fire lookout and Mount Jefferson, fewer than 7.0 miles distant, seems close enough you might get hit by rockfall from the summit.

The trail begins by gently climbing a rounded ridge through an evergreen forest, then dropping slightly to a saddle where the ridge rises sharply to the southeast, 0.6 mile from the trailhead. You'll round the ridge in the forest to the north, then contour underneath the ridge on a

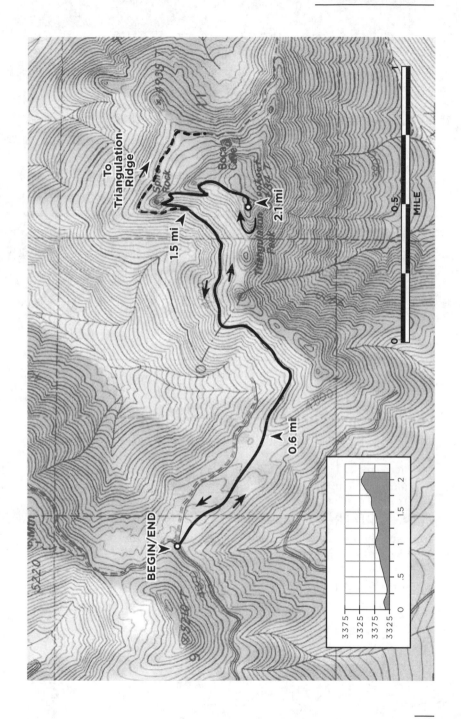

The vista of Mount Jefferson from the Triangulation Peak trail.

climbing traverse. The route continues to climb steadily but gently to a trail junction 1.5 miles from the trailhead, where the trail to the left leads around Spire Rock. Turn right at this junction and begin a series of steep switchbacks up the north ridge of Triangulation Peak, eventually walking directly up the ridge to the 5,434-foot summit. Climb over several large boulders for the best view of Mount Jefferson.

A steep, rocky trail leads downhill from the main trail to Boca Cave, a wet, mossy hole in the rock with its own view of Jefferson.

GOING FARTHER

You can add another 2 miles, one-way, to your hike by returning to the Spire Rock trail junction and turning right, circling Spire Rock and contouring around Triangulation Peak to walk the crest of the ridge, in and out of the forest, to the east.

53. Marion Lake

RATING	🚶 🚶 🚶 🚶
DISTANCE	5.2 miles round-trip
HIKING TIME	3 hours, 30 minutes
ELEVATION GAIN	670 feet
HIGH POINT	4,180 feet
EFFORT	Prepare to Perspire
BEST SEASON	Summer, fall
PERMITS/CONTACT	Northwest Forest Pass required; self-issue Wilderness Permit required/Willamette National Forest, (503) 854-3366
MAPS	USGS Marion Forks, Marion Lake
NOTES	Bicyclists and leashed dogs welcome; great family walk; very hot in summer

THE HIKE

Climb through the forest past a scenic subalpine lake to a larger lake with a loop trail and great views of Three Fingered Jack from the lakeshore.

GETTING THERE

Follow Oregon Highway 22 southeast from Detroit for 15.6 miles to Marion Forks and turn left on the Marion Lake Road (Forest Road 2255). Follow FR 2255 for 5 miles to the trailhead and road end, 3,380 feet above sea level. GPS trailhead coordinates: N44°34.606´; W121°53.634´

THE TRAIL

This is a very popular hike in the summer, one that I appreciated all the more because I'm older than glacier ice, therefore able to trek on weekdays. If you are enjoying that same circumstance, happy trails; if not, join the weekenders and take this walk anyway. It's a splendid hike.

The trail begins with a gentle traverse through the forest above the parking area, climbing above chattering Moon Creek, gradually gaining elevation as it enters the Mount Jefferson Wilderness about 0.8 mile from the trailhead. The forest grows older here and the route curves to the east, passing several small springs on turnpiked trail. Just beyond, at 0.9 mile, the trail gets steeper and switches back three times to climb

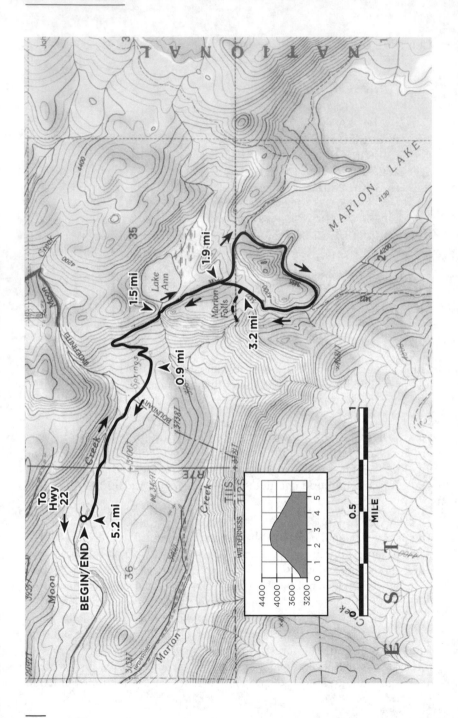

The trail to Marion Lake passes Lake Ann, a good stop for families with young children.

the hillside. Light breaks through the forest from a saddle in the ridge, as does the chatter of the creek that drains Lake Ann, 1.5 miles from the trailhead. Lake Ann might make an excellent picnic and turnaround spot for families with young children.

Cross the outlet stream at Lake Ann on boulders and follow the rocky west shore of Lake Ann for several hundred feet, then turn uphill through a swale to a junction with the Marion Outlet Trail, 1.9 miles from the trailhead. Keep left, round a hillside, and descend to the northwest end of Marion Lake, where the views of Three Fingered Jack dominate the skyline. The trail forks at the lakeshore and you'll turn right, following the trail around a peninsula to the southwest. The route circles above the lake outlet, which might be a good picnic spot, then climbs to the northwest to a junction with a side trail to the left, leading 0.1 mile to a viewpoint of Marion Falls. Beyond the junction, you'll climb another 0.1 mile to the junction with the main trail. To return to the trailhead, turn left and descend 1.9 miles.

GOING FARTHER

You can add another 2 miles, round-trip, by turning left at the lakeshore and walking southeast to the southern end of the lake on a trail that eventually climbs away from the lake, serving up views of the valley below.

54. Square Lake

RATING	🚶 🚶 🚶 🚶
DISTANCE	4.0 miles round-trip
HIKING TIME	2 hours
ELEVATION GAIN	180 feet
HIGH POINT	5,000 feet
EFFORT	Moderate Workout
BEST SEASON	Summer, fall
PERMITS/CONTACT	Northwest Forest Pass required; self-issue Wilderness Permit required/Deschutes National Forest, (541) 549-7700
MAPS	USGS Three Fingered Jack
NOTES	Leashed dogs welcome

THE HIKE

Here's a marvelous hike to a high alpine lake with a splendid view of Mount Washington and a chance to cool off with a swim.

GETTING THERE

From Sisters, drive northwest on U.S. Highway 20 for 12 miles to just past the summit of Santiam Pass and turn right onto the paved road to the Pacific Crest Trail No. 2000 trailhead, 4,840 feet above sea level. GPS trailhead coordinates: N44°25.561′; W121°50.991′

THE TRAIL

Portions of this trail pass through the lodgepole pine and subalpine fir forests damaged or destroyed by the B&B Complex Fire of 2003, the biggest wildfire in the history of Deschutes National Forest. The blaze burned more than 90,000 acres and killed half the trees across the affected area, costing $38 million to suppress. Reminders of the blaze are everywhere.

This hike can be hot in the summer, so you'll want to carry plenty of water or a good filter pump for the lake water. Bugs can be a distracting nuisance in the early summer so if you can wait until the first killing frost in the fall to take this hike, you'll enjoy it more. Begin by walking north on the Pacific Crest Trail for 0.2 mile to the Square Lake Trail. Turn right and follow the trail as it gradually climbs along the south-facing

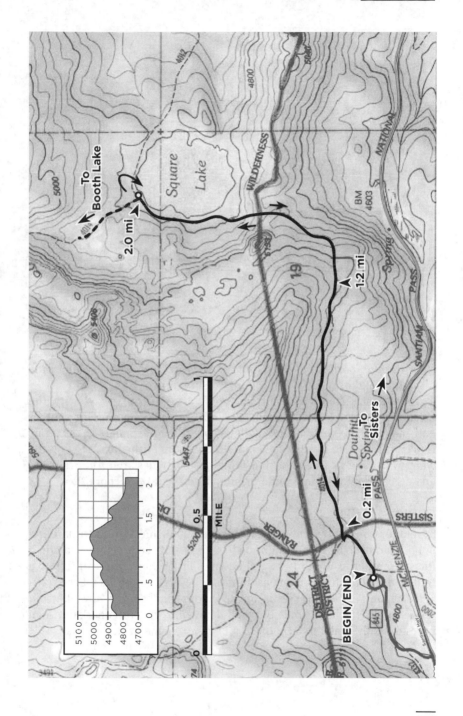

The trail to Square Lake provides a view of Mount Washington through burned forest.

slope through portions of the dying forest, with views to the south of the black lava and blasted face of Mount Washington.

At **1.2** miles from the trailhead, you'll begin a broad swing to the north, leaving the sound of Highway 20 behind and climbing for another half-mile to a 5,000-foot-high saddle overlooking the Square Lake cirque. Descend from here another half-mile to the shore of the lake, circling the water on the west side to a trail junction, **2.0** miles from the trailhead and a good spot to turn around or jump into the lake to cool off.

GOING FARTHER

Several options for extending your hike are available at your turnaround point. The most attractive might be to turn left at the junction and climb the steep gully to Booth Lake and beyond. From there, you can follow a trail to the north for as many as 4 miles, one-way, to the Jack Lake trailhead of the Pacific Crest Trail. For a shorter extension, follow the trail to the right, which descends in a half-mile, one-way, to Long Lake, then beyond another mile to a trailhead and campground at Round Lake.

55. Wasco Lake

RATING	🚶 🚶 🚶 🚶
DISTANCE	4.6 miles round-trip
HIKING TIME	3 hours
ELEVATION GAIN	420 feet
HIGH POINT	5,300 feet
FFFORT	Moderate Workout
BEST SEASON	Summer, fall
PERMITS/CONTACT	Northwest Forest Permit required; self-issue Wilderness Permit required/Deschutes National Forest, (541) 549-7700
MAPS	USGS Marion Lake, Three Fingered Jack
NOTES	Leashed dogs welcome

THE HIKE

Hike from remnants of an alpine forest through meadows to a classic alpine cirque and lake under the shadow of Three Fingered Jack.

GETTING THERE

From Sisters, follow U.S. Highway 20 west for 12.4 miles to Forest Road 12, signed "Mount Jefferson Wilderness Trailheads," and turn right. Follow FR 12 for 3.8 miles to a junction with Forest Road 1230 and turn left. Drive 1.5 miles to Forest Road 1234 and turn left. This rough road climbs steeply for 5 miles to the Jack Lake trailhead and campground, 5,147 feet above sea level. GPS trailhead coordinates: N44°29.503′; W121°47.650′

THE TRAIL

Begin by hiking around pretty little Jack Lake and its great alpine auto campground on the Wasco Lake Trail to the south and east. This section of the hike traverses some of the 90,000 acres of forest destroyed in the 2003 B&B Complex Fire. You'll climb briefly to a junction with the Canyon Creek Meadows Trail, 0.4 mile from the trailhead. Stay right and continue your gentle climb around a ridge to the east before contouring to Canyon Creek and its waterfall and junction with a trail descending from Canyon Creek Meadows.

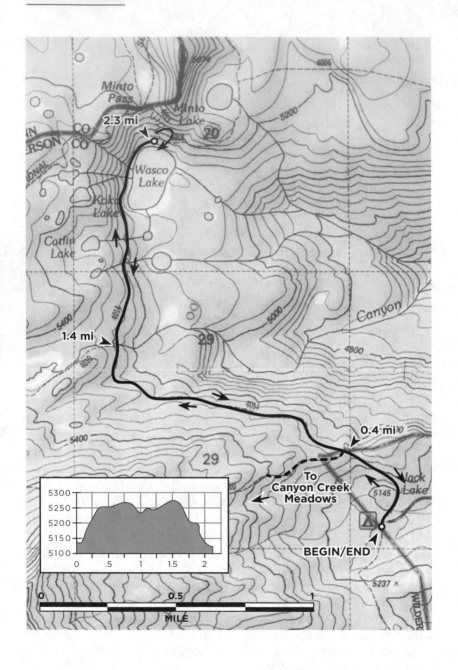

Dogs enjoy the water of Jack Lake at the Wasco Lake trailhead.

Stay right at this junction and continue around a wide ridge, crossing several streams that lead to mountain tarns both above and below the trail. The second of these creeks tumbles out of Carlin Lake, above. From here, you'll traverse into the cirque that hides Wasco Lake, the largest of a group of alpine tarns and lakes in the basin. Hike around the west side of the lake to a trail junction climbing steeply up to Minto Pass, your turnaround point at 2.3 miles from the trailhead.

GOING FARTHER

If you're looking for a more strenuous addition to this hike, turn left and climb the steep switchbacks leading to Minto Pass, named in 1874 after pioneer John Minto. The route then joins with the Pacific Crest Trail, which you can follow north to Canada or until you drop in an exhausted heap, ready to overdose on ibuprofen.

56. Canyon Creek Loop

RATING	🚶 🚶 🚶 🚶 🚶
DISTANCE	4.1 miles round-trip
HIKING TIME	2 hours, 30 minutes
ELEVATION GAIN	480 feet
HIGH POINT	5,750 feet
EFFORT	Moderate Workout
BEST SEASON	Summer, fall
PERMITS/CONTACT	Northwest Forest Permit required; self-issue Wilderness Permit required/Deschutes National Forest, (541) 549-7700
MAPS	USGS Marion Lake, Three Fingered Jack
NOTES	Leashed dogs welcome

THE HIKE

Walk through flowered meadows and burned forest to a beautiful alpine meadow with a view of Three Fingered Jack.

GETTING THERE

From Sisters, follow U.S. Highway 20 west for 12.4 miles to Forest Road 12, signed "Mount Jefferson Wilderness Trailheads," and turn right. Follow FR 12 for 3.8 miles to a junction with Forest Road 1230 and turn left. Drive 1.5 miles to Forest Road 1234 and turn left. This rough road climbs steeply for 5 miles to the Jack Lake trailhead and campground, 5,147 feet above sea level. GPS trailhead coordinates: N44°29.503´; W121°47.650´

THE TRAIL

The trail to Canyon Creek Meadows starts at what has to be one of the prettiest little auto campgrounds in Oregon at Jack Lake. Nearly a mile above sea level, your hike begins on the Wasco Lake Trail, which circles tiny Jack Lake in fire-killed forest to the east and south of the lake, and at **0.4** mile strikes a junction with the Canyon Creek Meadows Trail. Turn left and begin a steady, moderate climb up a wide ridge to a point where it grows steep, then descend on a traverse along the north-facing ridge into the meadows at Canyon Creek, **1.9** miles from the trailhead.

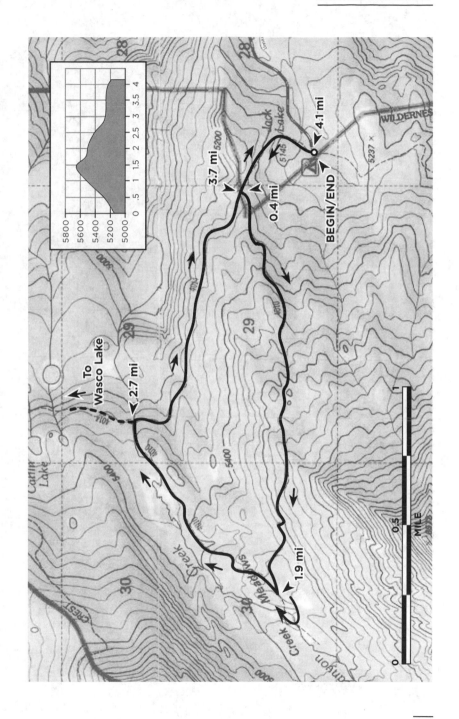

Hikers head down the trail to Canyon Creek Meadows.

You'll find trails heading both up and downstream at this point. For a great picnic and turnaround spot, head upstream for 0.2 mile to the meadow flats. The meadows offer a spectacular view of Three Fingered Jack, a sharp glaciated peak supposedly named after a trapper who only had three fingers and was called—I have it on the best authority—Margaret. When you're ready to hike back, return to the junction and keep to the left, following Canyon Creek downstream for 0.8 mile to rejoin the Wasco Lake Trail, 2.7 miles from the trailhead.

Turn right and follow the trail as it drops around a ridge to the east, then turns downhill to close the loop, 3.7 miles from the trailhead. Continue south and west around Jack Lake for 0.4 mile to the trailhead.

GOING FARTHER

The best way to extend this hike is to combine it with the hike to Wasco Lake and beyond. Wasco Lake is 1.8 round-trip miles beyond the junction with the upper Canyon Creek Meadows trail.

57. Black Butte

RATING	🚶 🚶 🚶 🚶 🚶
DISTANCE	4.0 miles round-trip
HIKING TIME	3 hours, 30 minutes
ELEVATION GAIN	1,550 feet
HIGH POINT	6,436 feet
EFFORT	Knee-Punishing
BEST SEASON	Fall
PERMITS/CONTACT	Northwest Forest Pass required/Deschutes National Forest, (541) 549-7700
MAPS	USGS Black Butte
NOTES	Leashed dogs welcome

THE HIKE

This tough climb is worth the effort for the 360-degree view you'll get of most of Oregon, Washington, Idaho, California, and points beyond—or at least it will seem that way on a clear day.

GETTING THERE

From Sisters, follow U.S. Highway 20 west for 6 miles to Green Ridge Road (Forest Road 11), then turn right and drive 3.8 miles to Forest Road 1110. Turn left on FR 1110 and drive 4.2 miles to Forest Road 700. Turn right and drive 1.1 miles on rocky, rutted FR 700 to a large parking area and trailhead, 4,880 feet above sea level. GPS trailhead coordinates: N44°23.719′; W121°38.899′

THE TRAIL

The hike to the summit of 6,436-foot-high Black Butte can be exhausting, not necessarily because of the continuous grade, but from the typically hot and dry weather through most of the summer. For this reason, it's best to take this hike later in the fall or as early as possible in the morning. An evening hike would be another possibility, but make sure you've enough light left to get down the trail. No matter what time you hike, carry double your regular water supply.

On the day I hiked this trail in August 2009, I met more than a dozen members of the Appalachian Mountain Club, a group of mostly retired

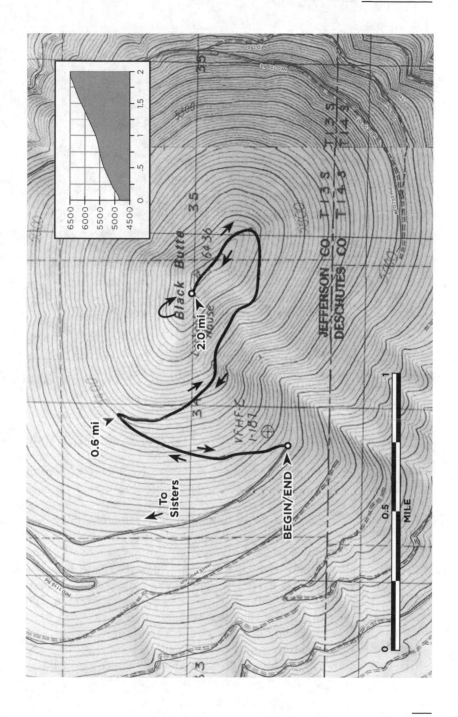

Members of the Appalachian Mountain Club's annual August Camp on the trail to Black Butte.

folk from the northeastern states who dashed up and down Black Butte as if it were a Sunday stroll. The hikers were part of the 65 club members hiking, bicycling, paddling, and enjoying the great outdoors of Central Oregon on the club's annual August Camp. The hike leader that day was 74 years old.

Begin by climbing stairs at the beginning of the hike onto a trail where handrails make excellent props over which to collapse on the return trip, but which were installed to keep hikers from cutting switchbacks. The trail starts climbing immediately at a moderate and even grade that continues throughout the entire 2.0 miles to the summit. You'll climb through a forest with peekaboo views through the pines along the western side of the butte, a volcanic cinder cone that sprouts 3,000 vertical feet from the forest floor. At **0.6** mile from the trailhead, the trail makes a single switchback and continues to climb relentlessly to the southeast.

The forest opens as you climb higher and the big ponderosas of lower elevation give way to shorter whitebark pine. As the view continues to expand, about 200 feet below the summit you'll make a broad switch-back and climb to the summit to the northwest. Several Forest Service lookouts occupy the summit, including the newest and still-working fire watchtower and a private residence for the lookout staff. The view from the summit is unbeatable, with Mount Washington and Three Fingered Jack closest to the north and the Three Sisters to the south.

GOING FARTHER
If you're ready to go farther after returning to the parking area, you're ready to trot up and down the Grand Canyon.

58. West Metolius River

RATING	𝕏 𝕏 𝕏
DISTANCE	4.5 miles round-trip
HIKING TIME	2 hours, 30 minutes
ELEVATION GAIN	120 feet
HIGH POINT	2,890 feet
EFFORT	Easy Walk
BEST SEASON	Fall
PERMITS/CONTACT	Northwest Forest Pass required/Deschutes National Forest, (541) 549-7700
MAPS	USGS Black Butte, Candle Creek, Prairie Farm Spring
NOTES	Leashed dogs welcome; great family hike

THE HIKE

This trail, popular with anglers, follows the spring-fed Metolius River downstream for 2.25 miles to the Wizard Falls Fish Hatchery.

GETTING THERE

Drive 10 miles west from Sisters on U.S. Highway 20 to the Camp Sherman Road (Forest Road 14) and turn right. Follow FR 14 for 2.7 miles to Forest Road 1419 and turn left. Follow FR 1419 for 2.3 miles to an intersection and stop sign, cross the road to Forest Road 1420, and follow FR 1420 for 3.4 miles to Forest Road 400. Turn right on FR 400 and follow it 0.9 mile to the Canyon Creek Campground and trailhead, 2,890 feet above sea level. GPS trailhead coordinates: N44°30.080′; W121°38.453′

THE TRAIL

The surprising clarity of the Metolius River is due to two facts: the water is filtered through volcanic rock and soil, literally springing from the ground; and it flows over that same lava rock, with little soil to erode. It's a fantastic river for fly-fishing and feeds fine, clear Lake Billy Chinook, where you can catch a variety of trout species as well as Atlantic salmon.

The trail never strays far from the west bank of the river as it winds through a forest of proud ponderosa pine trees decorated by an understory of purple lupine and thistle, columbine, and honeysuckle. At **0.2**

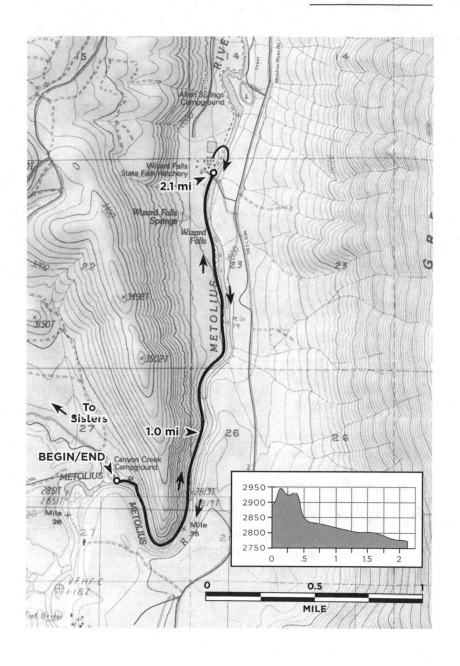

The Metolius River is a spring-fed stream of unusual clarity.

mile from the trailhead, you'll pass one of the springs that spills into the Metolius across the river. The route downstream drops gently through the forest, alternately passing the pools and riffles that attract anglers (and trout).

Continue downstream along the riverbank, reaching Wizard Falls at 2.1 miles and your turnaround point at Wizard Falls Fish Hatchery at 2.25 miles from the trailhead. This hatchery should be an especially fascinating spot for youngsters.

GOING FARTHER

It is possible to follow the trail for more than 4 miles, one-way, downstream from the hatchery. Trails continue downstream on either side of the river, which can be crossed at the hatchery bridge.

59. Deschutes River Reach

RATING	🏃 🏃
DISTANCE	5.0 miles round-trip
HIKING TIME	2 hours, 30 minutes
ELEVATION GAIN	175 feet
HIGH POINT	3,600 feet
EFFORT	Moderate Workout
BEST SEASON	Spring, fall
PERMITS/CONTACT	None/Bend Park and Recreation District, (541) 389-7275
MAPS	USGS Bend
NOTES	Leashed dogs and mountain bicyclists welcome

THE HIKE

Walk downstream through pine forest along the tumbling Deschutes River, in the middle of a city on a trail that feels like you're in the wild woods.

GETTING THERE

From U.S. Highway 97 in Bend, follow Division Street to NW Portland Avenue, turn right, and cross the bridge to First Street. Turn right on First and follow it to its end at First Street Rapids Park, 3,558 feet above sea level. GPS trailhead coordinates: N44°04.046´; W121°18.830´

THE TRAIL

This is a local favorite, where most of the skinny population of Bend goes at one time or another to jog, ride a bike, run flat out, cast a fly, watch birds, or perhaps even try to find errant golf balls from the River's Edge Golf Course. It may be worth noting here that much of the skinny population of Bend is not responsible for the errant golf balls, else they wouldn't be so skinny.

The wide trail drops to the river bank and heads north under a steep hillside, where birds and ground squirrels enjoy each other's company and appear to be as interested in the passing people as the people are in them. The river runs quickly here, tumbling over rapids before rounding a wide bend to the east, **0.6** mile from the trailhead. You'll cross a

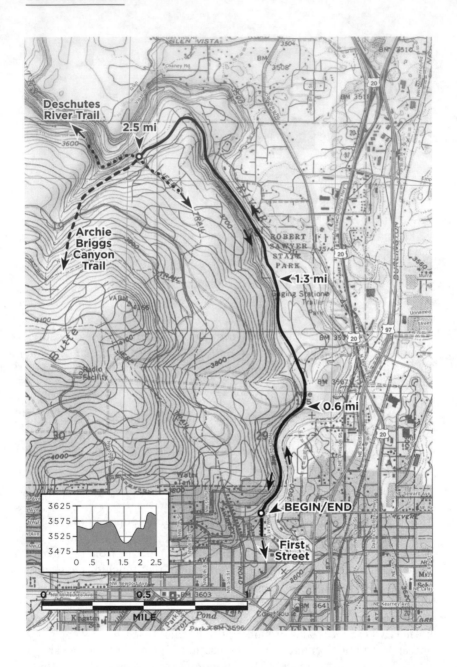

A jogger sets off down the Deschutes River Reach trail.

flat bench and Mount Washington Drive at **0.8** mile, paralleling the golf course for a distance. The trail follows the drive on either side before striking off on its own along the border of Sawyer Park, **1.3** miles from the trailhead, a favorite section for bird-watchers. It climbs above the canyon and crosses Archie Briggs Road at **2.0** miles from the trailhead and intersects the Archie Briggs Canyon Trail, your turnaround point, **2.5** miles from the trailhead.

GOING FARTHER

The trail climbs another 0.5 mile to the end, adding another mile to your round-trip. To add another round-trip mile, head up the Archie Briggs Canyon Trail and return.

60. Deschutes River Trail West

RATING	🚶 🚶
DISTANCE	6.2 miles round-trip
HIKING TIME	4 hours
ELEVATION GAIN	200 feet
HIGH POINT	3,975 feet
EFFORT	Moderate Workout
BEST SEASON	Fall
PERMITS/CONTACT	Northwest Forest Pass required/Deschutes National Forest, (541) 383-4000
MAPS	USGS Benham Falls
NOTES	Leashed dogs welcome; bicyclists welcome on some sections

THE HIKE

The walk along the Deschutes River passes through some of the country-side that basically remains unchanged from the time of the last volcanic activity, thousands of years ago.

GETTING THERE

Follow the Cascade Lakes Highway west from Bend to Forest Road 100, the Meadow Picnic Area, and turn left. Follow FR 100 past the southern end of a golf course and drop to the picnic area along the river 1.3 miles from the highway, 3,907 feet above sea level. GPS trailhead coordinates: N43°59.829′; W121°23.100′

THE TRAIL

The Deschutes River Trail stretches for miles along the river, with access points in downtown Bend and as distant as Sunriver and beyond. Not all sections of the path are completed yet, but each one offers a different perspective of one of the nicest waterways in Oregon for all forms of outdoor recreation.

The trail along most of this section offers hikers, equestrians, and mountain bicyclists the opportunity to enjoy themselves without worrying about one another: separate trails are provided along most of the way for each activity. This may be confusing at first; remember that the

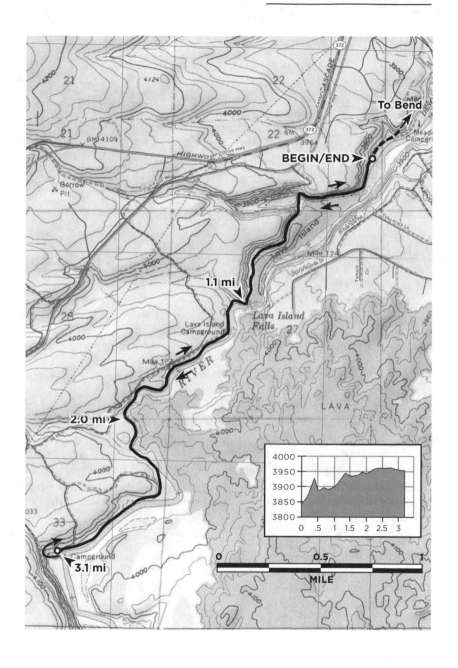

The Deschutes River Trail stretches for miles upstream from the Meadows trailhead.

pedestrian trails are always closest to the river and you won't have a problem.

The trail skirts Lava Island upstream from the Meadows trailhead, a part of the river that cut through an ancient lava flow, then drops back to the river at Lava Island Falls, 1.1 mile from the trailhead. Continue beyond, passing Lava Island Campground and following the river along grassy riverbank and ponderosa pine forest, winding to a wide bend to the south, where the trail crosses a peninsula and turns west once again for the final mile to the Aspen Campground, 3.1 miles from the trailhead.

GOING FARTHER
The best way to extend your hike is to follow the road and trail downstream from the Meadows trailhead to Benham Falls and beyond, adding up to 2 miles, one-way.

61. Todd Lake

RATING	🚶 🚶 🚶 🚶
DISTANCE	4.2 miles round-trip
HIKING TIME	2 hours, 30 minutes
ELEVATION GAIN	650 feet
HIGH POINT	6,680 feet
EFFORT	Prepare to Perspire
BEST SEASON	Summer, fall
PERMITS/CONTACT	Northwest Forest Pass required/Deschutes National Forest, (541) 383-4000
MAPS	USGS Broken Top
NOTES	Leashed dogs welcome

THE HIKE

Climb through forest over a low pass, then descend into alpine meadows filled with wildflowers and spectacular views.

GETTING THERE

From Bend, drive 27 miles west on the Cascade Lakes Highway to the Todd Lake Road (Forest Road 370) and turn right. Drive 0.6 mile to the large parking area and trailhead, 6,126 feet above sea level. GPS trailhead coordinates: N44°01.391'; W121°40.968'

THE TRAIL

If there's a single downside to this hike, it is the squadrons of biting flies and mosquitoes—some large enough to swoop down and grab Fido or little Missy—that wait in the mountains of Central Oregon. They hide there in tunnel systems, not unlike Afghan terrorists, to bite and suck the life out any warm-blooded creature that ventures near. Still, it is worth slathering yourself in DEET—worth returning from your hike resembling a massive mosquito bite with eyes and feet—to climb past the splendid view at Todd Lake to an even better view at the turnaround point. Another option would be to wait until the first frost in the mountains, which generally arrives earlier at this lofty elevation, for a nice reduced-bug autumn hike.

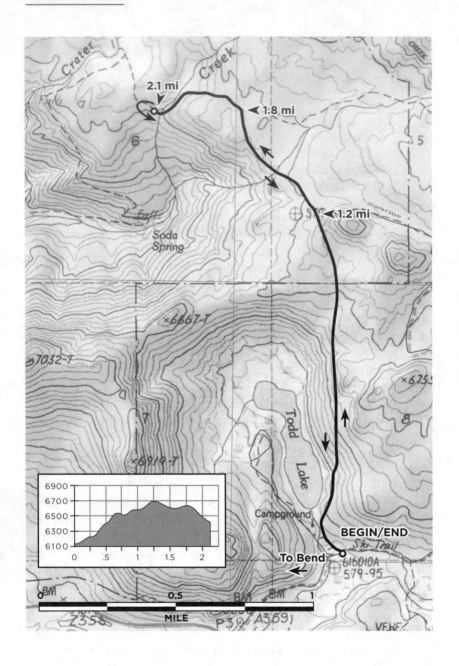

Broken Top overlooks Todd Lake, but the view gets better up the trail.

In either case, lace up those Vibrams and hit the trail, which climbs in a broad lane around the pretty Todd Lake outlet cascade and passes an interpretive sign that explains some of the history of the area. The trail crests the ridge and forks, with the left branch heading around the west side of the lake to walk-in campsites. Take the path to the right, which descends to a splendid view of Todd Lake from the forested saddle you'll shortly climb and the tip of 9,175-foot Broken Top beyond. The trail begins climbing immediately on a steady, moderately steep grade.

You'll stay in a forest of fir and hemlock, which shutters the view down to the lake, as the trail climbs nearly 300 feet in the first 0.4 mile. The grade eases a bit and passes a rounded peak to the east, where it joins a trail heading to the east at 1.2 miles. This trail leads to an abandoned road which eventually circles back to Todd Lake, but you'll continue to the left and begin a descending traverse. Cross a fork of Soda Creek and, at 1.8 miles from the trailhead, find an intersection with the Soda Creek Trail. Keep left here and descend another 0.3 mile to open meadows where the trail crosses Soda Creek. This is your turnaround point, an excellent picnic spot with a view of Broken Top and the Green Lakes Basin.

GOING FARTHER

For a longer hike, continue another 0.3 mile to a junction with a trail that climbs left to a view of the falls at Soda Springs, 1.1 miles, one-way, from the turnaround point. You can also descend past this junction into the beautiful Green Lakes Basin, an option that could add as many as 3 or 4 miles, one-way, to your hike.

62. Smith Rock

RATING	🚶 🚶 🚶
DISTANCE	4.0 miles round-trip
HIKING TIME	2 hours, 30 minutes
ELEVATION GAIN	320 feet
HIGH POINT	2,840 feet
EFFORT	Moderate Workout
BEST SEASON	Spring, fall
PERMITS/CONTACT	Day Use Permit required/Smith Rock State Park, (541) 923-7551
MAPS	USGS Redmond
NOTES	Leashed dogs welcome; bicyclists and equestrians welcome on some trails

THE HIKE

Wildlife viewing is likely to play second fiddle to rock climber viewing on this walk along the Crooked River, with the option of a rock scramble over Asterisk Pass.

GETTING THERE

From U.S. Highway 97 in Terrebonne, turn east and follow the signs 3.4 miles to Smith Rock State Park, where you'll be asked to buy a Day Use Permit ($3 in 2009) from a machine in the parking area, 2,840 feet above sea level. GPS trailhead coordinates: N44º22.025'; W121º08.156'

THE TRAIL

The incredible scenery at Smith Rock may not be important to the majority of this state park's users, who visit to climb the chimneys, cracks, and smooth vertical walls of rhyolite. That should be of little importance to you, however, because the climbers simply add to the drama and color of the vistas. The rock towers above while splendid Crooked River slides alongside the trail, bringing life to the permanent residents of Smith Rock: golden eagles, falcons, Canada geese, and a variety of reptiles, including rattlesnakes.

Find the service road that descends into the Crooked River Canyon at the trailhead and hike down to the river, either on the gentle equestrian

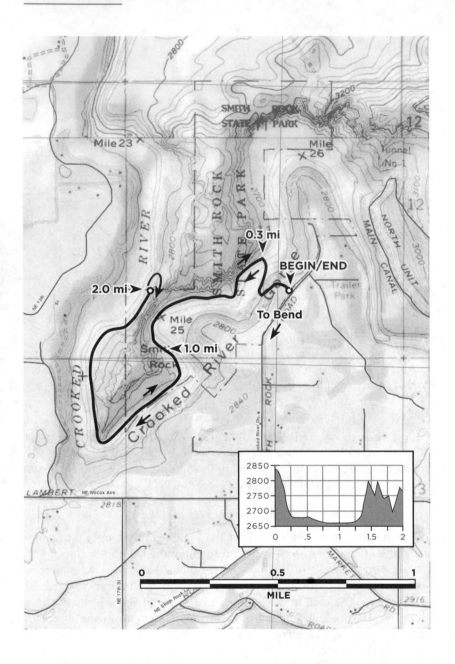

Hikers head down the Smith Rock trail for a picnic.

trail or the steeper pedestrian route, to a footbridge crossing Crooked River, 0.3 mile from the trailhead. You'll find a drinking fountain and outhouse at the bridge. Just across the bridge, you'll arrive at a trail junction. Turn left and follow the trail as it goes along the river downstream at the base of cliffs where climbers' paths lead to rocks named Picnic Lunch Wall, Morning Glory Wall, and the Dihedrals. The trail winds past a horse ford to the east at 1.0 mile from the trailhead and follows the river as it meanders around a wide bend to the southwest.

The trail stays near the rock and rounds a sharp point as the river turns to the north and the trail meanders away from the river on flats that make a good picnic area and turnaround point, 2.0 miles from the trailhead. Return the way you came, or if you'd like an absolutely frightening experience, follow the obvious climber's shortcut over Asterisk Pass. It was at this very spot that I told my wife, B. B. Hardbody, that if I survived the climb I would never do anything stupid again. She just laughed and scrambled like a spider up and over the rock while I clung to the rock like a petrified slug. It is interesting to note that while I quivered there, a *real* rock climber passed me on the outside in his bare feet, his rock shoes swinging around his neck.

As you can probably guess, I did survive the climb, but I have not lived up to my promise. Indeed, I've done many stupid things since my climb over Asterisk Pass. Also, before attempting this rock scramble, you should be aware that Oregon State Parks recommends using a rope.

GOING FARTHER

You can continue on the trail for another mile to a junction with a trail that climbs in steep switchbacks for 500 feet to the east over Misery Ridge. Once there, you can walk out on a short trail to the edge of a cliff that looks directly into the "mouth" of Monkey Face, the 400-foot-high tower that is one of the most popular climbs at Smith Rock. Beyond the viewpoint, the trail switches back down to the Crooked River Bridge. This strenuous loop hike would be 4.8 miles.

63. Paulina Lake

RATING	🚶 🚶 🚶 🚶
DISTANCE	4.4 miles round-trip
HIKING TIME	2 hours, 30 minutes
ELEVATION GAIN	50 feet
HIGH POINT	6,380 feet
EFFORT	Easy Walk
BEST SEASON	Summer, fall
PERMITS/CONTACT	Northwest Forest Pass required/Deschutes National Forest, (541) 383-4000
MAPS	USGS East Lake, Paulina Peak
NOTES	Leashed dogs welcome; bicycles and horses prohibited

THE HIKE

Here's a scenic trek along the shoreline of Paulina Lake, a water-filled crater within the massive Newberry Crater.

GETTING THERE

Drive 23 miles south of Bend on U.S. Highway 97 and turn left on the Paulina Lake Road (Forest Road 21). Drive 11.6 miles to the Newberry Crater entrance booth, where you can pay a $10 fee for a 3-day pass or display your Northwest Forest Pass. Drive another 1.6 miles to the Paulina Lake Campground day use area on the left, 6,360 feet above sea level. GPS trailhead coordinates: N43°42.762′; W121°16.376′

THE TRAIL

This is a fascinating walk along the shoreline of a lake that was once part of a volcanic caldera that covers more than 17 square miles. Besides Paulina Lake, you'll find volcanic caves and tubes, cinder cones, and East Lake inside the Newberry Crater. The shoreline trail along Paulina Lake offers a quiet way to tour the area, where you can find wildflowers in season and see a variety of shorebirds and other wildlife. Black bears are an occasional nuisance in the campgrounds around the lake—count yourself fortunate if you see one.

The hike begins at the shoreline just east of the campground boat launch and circles to the southeast along the shoreline around a pair of

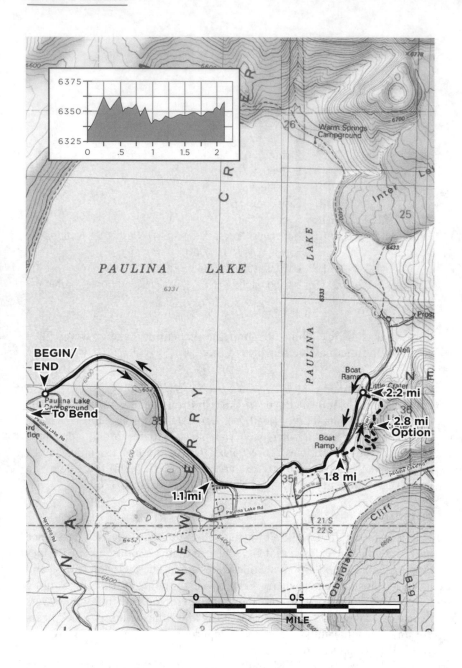

The Paulina Lake trail circles the lake.

forested hills. This section of trail is quiet and lonely, and on autumn weekdays you may not see another hiking party. At 1.1 miles, you'll walk past some private residences on leased forest land around a wide bay, passing another boat launch at the Little Crater Campground, 1.8 miles from the trailhead. You can cross the road here and follow the trail up and over Little Crater, a 6,535-foot-high cinder cone, descending the other side to the east end of Little Crater Campground, 2.8 miles from the trailhead. A gentler option is to follow the road and shoreline trail in front of the campground to the east end, your turnaround point 2.2 miles from the trailhead.

GOING FARTHER

The shoreline trail continues around the lake, making an 8.3-mile loop, rarely climbing more than 80 feet above the lake and passing two hike-in or boat-in campgrounds on the north side of the lake. The halfway point around the loop is the interesting Interlake Obsidian Flow, 2 miles north of the turnaround point. If you walk that far, follow the loop around the quieter side of Paulina Lake.

64. Chimney Rock

RATING	🚶 🚶
DISTANCE	2.6 miles round-trip
HIKING TIME	1 hour, 30 minutes
ELEVATION GAIN	540 feet
HIGH POINT	3,640 feet
EFFORT	Moderate Workout
BEST SEASON	Spring, fall
PERMITS/CONTACT	None/Ochoco National Forest, (541) 416-6500
MAPS	USGS Stearns Butte
NOTES	Leashed dogs welcome; extremely hot in summer

THE HIKE

This short trail takes you to a flat saddle below one of the most promi-
nent rocks in the Lower Crooked River Wild and Scenic Area, where
you'll get a melt-your-mind view of the river canyon and surrounding
country.

GETTING THERE

From Prineville, follow Main Street (Crooked River Highway 27) south
for 17.1 miles to the Chimney Rock trailhead, located on the east side of
the highway across from the entrance to the Chimney Rock Campground,
3,038 feet above sea level. GPS trailhead coordinates: N44°08.107′;
W120°48.785′

THE TRAIL

The view up and down the Crooked River from a bench overlooking the
river on a saddle below Chimney Rock is only one of the rewards you get
after making this hike's steady climb. Besides the view, you'll discover a
beautiful stretch of lonely highway that winds along the river past primitive riverside campgrounds that look positively desperate for company.
Sage and juniper color the canyon, a stark contrast to the forests of the
Cascades barely 40 miles west.

The trail begins climbing at the get-go, heading north to a switchback.
Climbing south now, the path is pocked by sharp basalt that could trip
you if your eyes, like mine, are glued on Chimney Rock to the south.

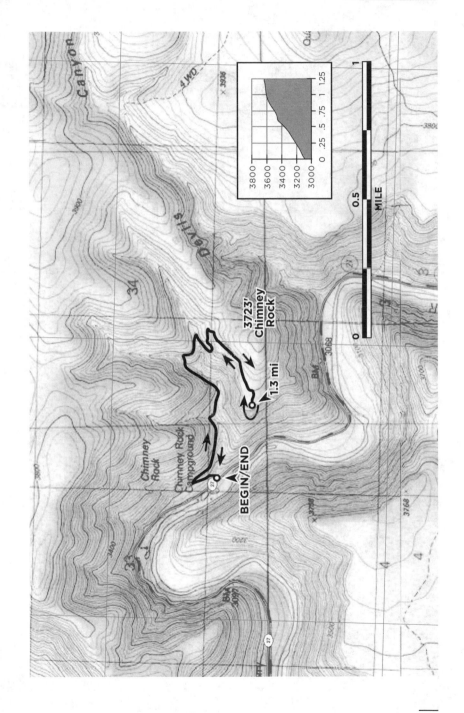

Chimney Rock from the trail.

I stumbled only a couple of times until I began watching where I was putting my feet. You'll climb to a rocky promontory, then follow a side canyon for a hundred yards, contouring to the east into a second, steeper canyon.

Climb up this rocky gulch and cross to the south side, where you'll encounter a couple of short, steep switchbacks underneath Devil's Ridge. Chimney Rock comes into view as you round a ridge and arrive at a bench, **1.0** mile from the trailhead. Once you've caught your breath, continue climbing another 0.3 mile to the end of the trail and a second bench at a saddle below Chimney Rock. From here you can see the curve and sweep of the Crooked River below and look west to the snowy Cascades.

GOING FARTHER
The best way to extend this hike would be to return to the trailhead and walk across the highway to the Chimney Rock Campground road, which follows the river downstream for 0.5 mile. An intermittent angler's trail continues along the river where the steep terrain permits.

Hoffer Lake lies under the peaks of the Elkhorn Crest.

DISTANT TRAILS

I made a mistake when I compiled the trails for the *Creaky Knees Guide Washington*. I included day hikes for trails that were so far from anywhere, it took longer than a day to get there. You, dear Oregon hiker, need not suffer from my mistake.

Indeed, I've listed a dozen hikes that are a long ways from most population centers. But they are incredible hikes, and clustered for the most part so that you can plan a weekend excursion, spending a night or two at a nearby campground and enjoying two or three of these outings with enough time left to get home to the Bengay before bedtime.

It's mainly interstate highway to the trails in the Wallowas and Elkhorn Crest, with campgrounds located at either destination. Hikes are clustered around the Anthony Lakes area, and if you don't want to camp, you can always find lodging in La Grande, North Powder, Joseph, or Baker City.

The rest of the hikes in this section are clustered around Crater Lake and splendid Diamond Lake, with its four campgrounds and resort. I hope you find something here that makes your trip worthwhile.

DISTANT TRAILS

65. Mount Howard

RATING	🚶 🚶 🚶 🚶 🚶
DISTANCE	2.0 miles round-trip
HIKING TIME	1 hour, 30 minutes
ELEVATION GAIN	80 feet
HIGH POINT	8,160 feet
EFFORT	Stroll in the Park
BEST SEASON	Summer
PERMITS/CONTACT	Tram ticket required/Wallowa-Whitman National Forest, (541) 426-5546
MAPS	USGS Joseph
NOTES	Leashed dogs and mountain bikes permitted; excellent family hike

THE HIKE

It isn't so much the views or exercise that should attract families with young children to this hike, but the great tramway ride to the plateau summit of Mount Howard. Youngsters will love it, while everyone else will be blown away by a vista that stretches across four states on a clear day.

GETTING THERE

From Joseph, follow Oregon Highway 82 along the shore of Wallowa Lake for 5.9 miles and turn left at the sign directing you to the gondola station. Drive 0.3 mile to the parking area and trailhead, 5,030 feet above sea level. GPS trailhead coordinates: N45°16.631´; W117°12.420´

THE TRAIL

Here's an idea: you can truthfully tell friends and neighbors that you climbed an 8,256-foot mountain in a matter of minutes. You don't have to tell them you did it by riding a gondola that whisks you to the top of Mount Howard, climbing 3,700 feet in 1.8 miles from the shores of Wallowa Lake on one of the steepest trams in North America. Adult tickets cost $24 in 2009 (senior, $21; ages 4–11, $14). The sweeping view from the summit is proclaimed to be the "best in Oregon," not surprisingly by the folks who run the tram. It's possible to argue the point, but it would

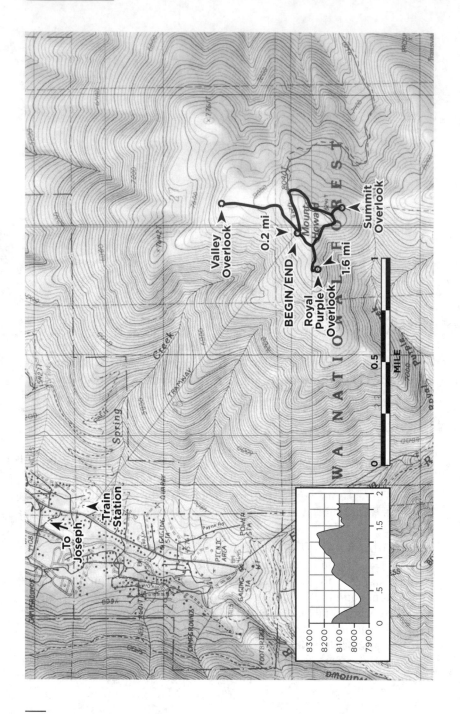

A hiker walks the trail around the summit of Mount Howard.

simply be a waste of time better spent by ogling the mountains and valleys of the Eagle Cap Wilderness, the Blue Mountains, and beyond. On
clear days in early summer, you can see snowcapped peaks in Montana,
Idaho, and Washington.

Several hiker trails and mountain bike routes radiate from the tram's
summit station, but the best walk is the 2.0-mile loop that begins on a
trail that heads to the east from the summit station, yielding a clockwise loop around the summit plateau past side trails leading to several
overlooks. You'll first find the Valley Overlook, about 0.2 mile from the
summit station. From here, you can look into the Wallowa Valley and
Lake, 3,000 feet below, and north for miles to mountains in Idaho, Washington, and Montana.

Past the overlook, the route circles to the south around the actual summit of Mount Howard, the 8,165-foot knob on your right, to the Summit

Overlook. This high plateau, and much of the Wallowa Mountain alpine country, nurtures ancient whitebark pine, the gnarled trees that can live more than 1,000 years.

You'll continue on the trail, circling to the west and north, to the Royal Purple Viewpoint, named for the gold mine and creek in the valley below, about 1.6 miles from the summit station. After you've overloaded your senses with the views, walk back to the gondola for a picnic and ride down. The summit station has a café and gift shop.

GOING FARTHER
Hikers seeking more exercise will find several routes of varying lengths leading off Mount Howard, used primarily by mountain bikers. You can pick up a map and directions at the tram station.

66. Dutch Flat Trail

RATING	🚶 🚶
DISTANCE	6.0 miles round-trip
HIKING TIME	3 hours, 30 minutes
ELEVATION GAIN	600 feet
HIGH POINT	5,400 feet
EFFORT	Moderate Workout
BEST SEASON	Summer, fall
PERMITS/CONTACT	Northwest Forest Pass required/Wallowa-Whitman National Forest, (541) 523-4476
MAPS	USGS Anthony Lakes
NOTES	Leashed dogs welcome

THE HIKE

Here's a gentle hike along a tumbling creek to a long meadow with forested ridges and rocky summits rising on either side.

GETTING THERE

From Interstate 84 at North Powder, take exit 285 and follow the signs to Anthony Lakes via Country Road 101, Elkhorn Scenic Byway, and Forest Road 73 to its intersection with Forest Road 7307 and turn left. Follow FR 7307 for 1 mile to the Dutch Flat Trail No. 1607 trailhead, 4,992 feet above sea level. GPS trailhead coordinates: N44°57.756'; W118°07.040'

THE TRAIL

One of the nice things about this trail is that you're not as likely to have company—at least from humans—as you would be on other higher trails in the Elkhorn Crest area. This is a pleasant walk along the Dutch Flat Creek, underneath the steep Van Patten Butte to the north and the multiple peaks of Twin Mountain to the south. The valley is home to a variety of birds and other wildlife, including deer and elk.

The path climbs on a gentle grade through a spruce and pine forest, colored golden in the fall by the occasional larch. The trail never strays far from the creek, where a number of clearings in the forest invite hikers to stop short of the turnaround point at Dutch Flat Meadow. But the forest continues to open, and at **2.5 miles** you'll arrive at the beginning of

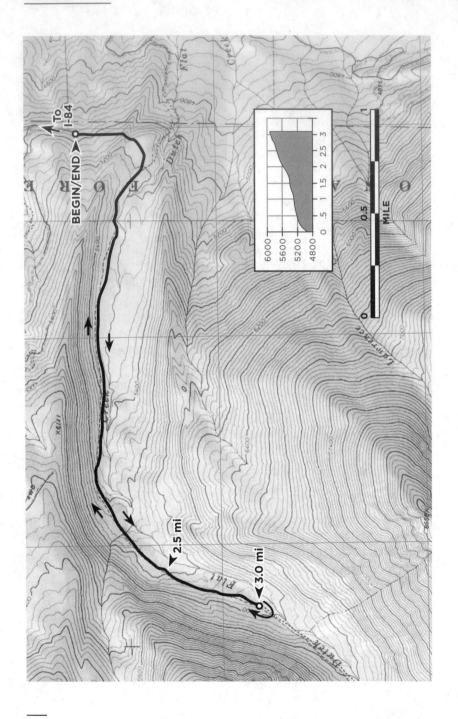

The Dutch Flat Trail begins on a forested hillside.

the long meadow. The trail continues past a number of inviting spots to stop at the edge of the forest, with one of the nicest areas at a wider part of the meadow, **3.0** miles from the trailhead. This is an excellent spot to settle, watch Dutch Flat Creek roll by, and silently congratulate Mother Nature for her excellent work.

GOING FARTHER

The meadow stretches for about another mile along the creek, then begins a steep, steady climb in switchbacks past a high meadow to Dutch Flat Lake, 7.1 miles from the trailhead. Assuming you're in prime condition and have plenty of anti-inflammatory pills in the first-aid kit, you can continue another steep, strenuous mile to Dutch Flat Saddle, 8,000 feet above sea level and 8.4 miles from the trailhead.

67. Elkhorn Crest

RATING	🚶 🚶 🚶
DISTANCE	5.8 miles round-trip
HIKING TIME	3 hours
ELEVATION GAIN	1,100 feet
HIGH POINT	8,180 feet
EFFORT	Knee-Punishing
BEST SEASON	Summer, fall
PERMITS/CONTACT	Northwest Forest Pass required/Wallowa-Whitman National Forest, (541) 523-4476
MAPS	USGS Anthony Lakes
NOTES	Leashed dogs welcome

THE HIKE

This tough climb leads to the spectacular alpine wilderness south of Anthony Lakes, high country dotted with clear lakes and teeming with wildlife.

GETTING THERE

From Interstate 84 at North Powder, take exit 285 and follow the signs to Anthony Lakes via County Road 101, Elkhorn Scenic Byway, and Forest Road 73 for 20 miles to the Elkhorn Crest trailhead, just east of the Anthony Lakes Campground, 7,100 feet above sea level. GPS trailhead coordinates: N44°57.775'; W118°13.540'

THE TRAIL

This is the most difficult of several hikes in the high country of the John Day Wilderness, a splendid piece of real estate still owned by Mother Nature and—since the whole thing is located within the boundaries of the Wallowa-Whitman National Forest—you. The Elkhorn Crest Trail, which stretches 28 miles south, is popular with equestrians, mountain bikers, and dirt bike riders, but at this end of the trail it is restricted to hikers and equestrians.

The trail ambles along a rounded ridge through meadows decorated by lodgepole and whitebark pine for 0.6 mile, where it intersects the Black Lake Trail. Stay left and climb for a hundred yards, where the Black Lake

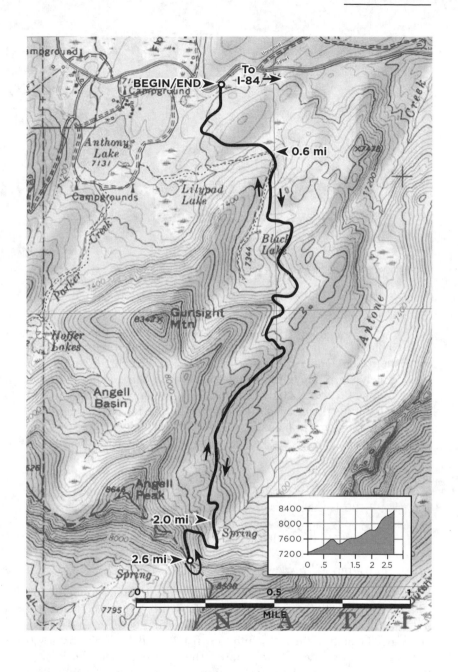

The Elkhorn Crest trail crosses a massive granite formation.

Trail climbs to the lake on the right. You'll continue climbing left on the Elkhorn Crest Trail, just east of the lake. The trail climbs steadily on a moderately steep grade, switching back several times along the ridge above Antone Creek. At 2.0 miles, you'll cross the only water on the trail at a small spring that may not be running in the fall. If you're hiking with children, this might make a good turnaround spot.

Beyond, the trail begins climbing more steeply, switches back twice above the Antone Creek headwaters, and angles toward an un-named pass just east of Angell Peak. The peak is 8,646 feet high and, like many of the northern crags of the Elkhorn Crest, is home to mountain goats. The pass, 8,180 feet above sea level, is a good spot to take a load off your barking dogs, enjoy the view, and steel yourself for the knee-jarring tromp back down to the trailhead.

GOING FARTHER

You can continue another 0.5 mile over the pass, dropping to a junction with trails leading to Dutch Flat Lake and Crawfish Meadows. The trail to Dutch Flat Lake, to the left, drops a joint-whacking 600 feet in 0.9 mile, one-way. The path to the right, into Crawfish Meadows, drops about 400 feet and contours above the meadows. This trail eventually leads back to the Anthony Lakes Campground, forming a strenuous 8.4-mile loop hike.

68. Black Lake

RATING	🚶 🚶 🚶
DISTANCE	2.0 miles round-trip
HIKING TIME	1 hour, 30 minutes
ELEVATION GAIN	250 feet
HIGH POINT	7,345 feet
EFFORT	Moderate Workout
BEST SEASON	Summer, fall
PERMITS/CONTACT	Northwest Forest Pass required/Wallowa-Whitman National Forest, (541) 523-4476
MAPS	USGS Anthony Lakes
NOTES	Leashed dogs welcome

THE HIKE

Here's a short hike to a nice alpine lake under the shadow of the Elkhorn Crest, the sharp, rocky spine of the John Day Wilderness.

GETTING THERE

From Interstate 84 at North Powder, take exit 285 and follow the signs to Anthony Lakes via Country Road 101, Elkhorn Scenic Byway, and Forest Road 73 to Forest Road 7300-710 at Anthony Lakes Campground. Turn left and follow FR 7300-710 past the campground to the boat launch and the Black Lake trailhead, 7,100 feet above sea level. GPS trailhead coordinates: N44°57.522'; W118°13.734'

THE TRAIL

This short hike climbs a bit into a marshy valley underneath the Elkhorn Crest for 0.5 mile above Lilypad Lake, which, as you might guess, is covered with water lily blossoms throughout the summer. The trail heads east above the lake, crossing a meadow at the end of the lake and climbing to a junction with the Elkhorn Crest Trail, 0.6 mile from the trailhead.

Turn right and follow the Elkhorn Crest Trail for several hundred feet, then look for the Black Lake Trail No. 1600 as it turns right, climbing along a ridge to a meadow and the outlet stream from Black Lake, which lies in a narrow valley below Gunsight Mountain. The lake is popular with anglers and backpackers looking for an easy getaway.

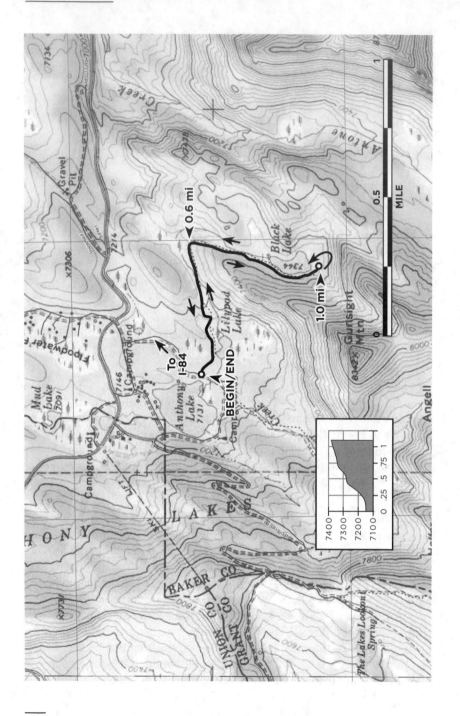

Lilypad Lake lies beside the trail to Black Lake.

69. Hoffer Lakes Loop

RATING	𐤀 𐤀 𐤀 𐤀
DISTANCE	2.0 miles round-trip
HIKING TIME	1 hour, 30 minutes
ELEVATION GAIN	300 feet
HIGH POINT	7,430 feet
EFFORT	Prepare to Perspire
BEST SEASON	Summer, fall
PERMITS/CONTACT	Northwest Forest Pass required/Wallowa-Whitman National Forest, (541) 523-4476
MAPS	USGS Anthony Lakes
NOTES	Leashed dogs welcome; great family hike

THE HIKE

Here's a fine loop hike past a nice alpine lake in the wild country around Anthony Lakes and the Elkhorn Crest.

GETTING THERE

From Interstate 84 at North Powder, take exit 285 and follow the signs to Anthony Lakes via Country Road 101, Elkhorn Scenic Byway, and Forest Road 73 to Forest Road 7300-710 at Anthony Lakes Campground. Turn into the campground and drive 0.3 mile to the day use area on the west shore of the lake at the end of the road, 7,150 feet above sea level. GPS trailhead coordinates: N44°57.504′; W118°14.026′

THE TRAIL

This hike is the best short walk in the Anthony Lakes area, circling a splendid alpine lake and traversing meadows alive with wildflowers in early summer. With the cloud-scratching crags of the Elkhorn Crest above, it is understandable why this area is so popular with anglers, equestrians, hunters, and, of course, wilderness pedestrians like you. On all of the hikes in this region, you'll likely recognize the fact that you're more than 7,000 feet above sea level. Though the grades are short, they'll seem longer because of the extreme altitude.

Begin by following the south shoreline of Anthony Lake along a wide path for 0.2 mile to a junction with the Hoffer Lake Trail No. 1604. Turn

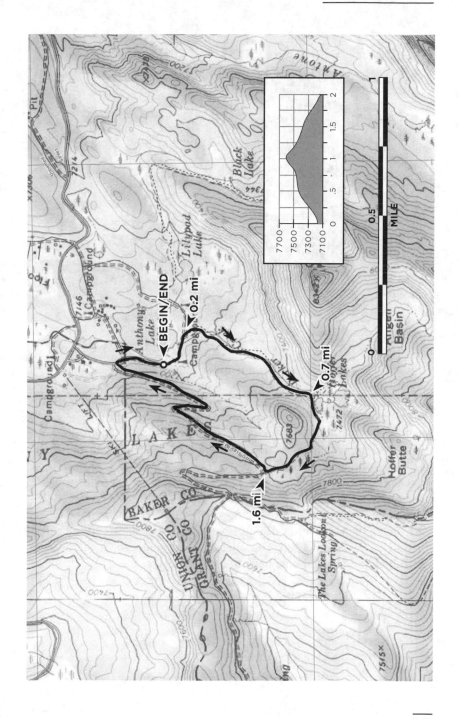

The Hoffer Lakes Loop trail crosses several footbridges like this.

right and begin a short, steep climb above Parker Creek in lodgepole pine and subalpine fir forest to the lake, **0.7** mile from the trailhead.

The trail now skirts a meadow along the smaller of the two Hoffer Lakes, where a waterfall cascades over the white granite that decorates much of the Elkhorns. The (barely) larger Hoffer Lake lies to the south, across a meadow that was deposited there thousands of years ago by the glacier that divided the once single Hoffer Lake. Of course, back in those days it wasn't known as Hoffer Lake—and, in fact, was probably not known at all.

Regardless, the trail follows the north shore of the smaller lake for 0.2 mile, then climbs in steps through several alpine meadows to the end of the trail on Forest Road 185, **1.6** miles from the trailhead. Turn right here and follow the road 0.4 mile back to Anthony Lake.

70. Crawfish Basin Trail

RATING	🚶 🚶 🚶
DISTANCE	4.0 miles round-trip
HIKING TIME	3 hours
ELEVATION GAIN	200 feet
HIGH POINT	7,800 feet
EFFORT	Moderate Workout
BEST SEASON	Summer, fall
PERMITS/CONTACT	Northwest Forest Pass required/Wallowa-Whitman National Forest, (541) 523-4476
MAPS	USGS Anthony Lakes
NOTES	Bicyclists and leashed dogs welcome; great family walk; very hot in summer

THE HIKE

This high alpine trail might be best of all for wildlife-watchers, especially those who are looking for mountain goats. Alpine scenery on this hike is spectacular.

GETTING THERE

From Interstate 84 at North Powder, take exit 285 and follow the signs to Anthony Lakes via Country Road 101, Elkhorn Scenic Byway, and Forest Road 73 past Elkhorn Summit. Turn left at Chicken Hill Road (Forest Road 210) and follow it to Forest Road 187, then follow Forest Road 187 south to the beginning of Crawfish Basin Trail No. 1612, 7,813 feet above sea level. GPS trailhead coordinates: N44°56.986'; W118°14.790'

THE TRAIL

This high trail begins at the crest of the Elkhorn Mountains, where the air is thin and the scenery unbeatable. It crosses the northeast portion of the North Fork John Day Wilderness and provides jaw-dropping views of Angell Peak above and Crawfish Basin below. The path contours under the crest of a rocky ridge that divides Anthony Lakes from the Crawfish Creek drainage. Hike to the southwest past a spring, then round a sharp ridge that climbs above to the Lakes Lookout, on the crest of the Anthony Lakes divide, 1.0 mile from the trailhead.

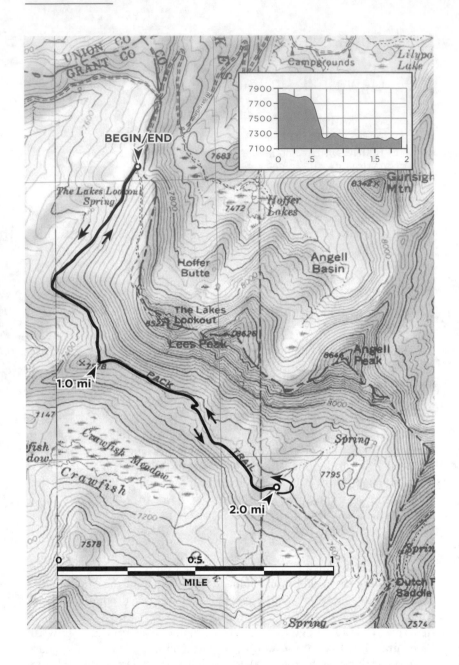

A "silver forest" above the Crawfish Basin Trail.

You'll turn toward the southeast here and begin a traverse above the Crawfish Basin, 400 feet below. The trail drops about 200 feet in the next mile, crossing a small creek that spills into the meadow from a tiny tarn above. This is a good spot to enjoy the view, try to spot mountain goats, and enjoy a picnic lunch, 2.0 miles from the trailhead.

GOING FARTHER
You can continue following Crawfish Basin Trail No. 1612 for another 0.6 mile, one-way, where it reaches the head of the basin and climbs in steep, short switchbacks for nearly 300 vertical feet to Dutch Flat Saddle. This saddle is located at the junction of four trails, including the Elkhorn Crest Trail. You can turn left on the Elkhorn Crest Trail and follow it back to the Black Lake Trail, turn left and pass Lilypad and Hoffer lakes to climb back to the trailhead. That would make a strenuous loop hike of 8.4 miles.

71. Crawfish Lake

RATING	🚶 🚶
DISTANCE	2.5 miles round-trip
HIKING TIME	2 hours
ELEVATION GAIN	300 feet
HIGH POINT	7,200 feet
EFFORT	Moderate Workout
BEST SEASON	Summer, fall
PERMITS/CONTACT	Northwest Forest Pass required/Wallowa-Whitman National Forest, (541) 523-4476
MAPS	USGS Crawfish Lake
NOTES	Leashed dogs welcome

THE HIKE

The short hike to a scenic little lake might seem easy at first, since it begins with a downhill romp. Keep that in mind as you sweat back up to the trailhead on your return.

GETTING THERE

From Interstate 84 at North Powder, take exit 285 and follow the signs to Anthony Lakes via Country Road 101, Elkhorn Scenic Byway, and Forest Road 73, passing the Anthony Lakes Ski Area and crossing the Elkhorn Crest to Forest Road 7300-216, signed "Crawfish Lake." Turn left and drive 0.2 mile to the trailhead, 7,207 feet above sea level. GPS trailhead coordinates: N44°57.038'; W118°15.912'

THE TRAIL

This walk begins with a steep downhill passage on Forest Trail 1606 through a pine forest burned by several wildfires of the past, including a 1986 blaze and a previous fire in the early '60s. Backpackers and hunters sometimes use the route as access to the North Fork John Day Wilderness and Elkhorn Range.

The route crosses open slopes decorated with lupine and paintbrush for the first 0.5 mile before entering the forest, where the trail drops at a more moderate grade before climbing briefly into the glacial basin that

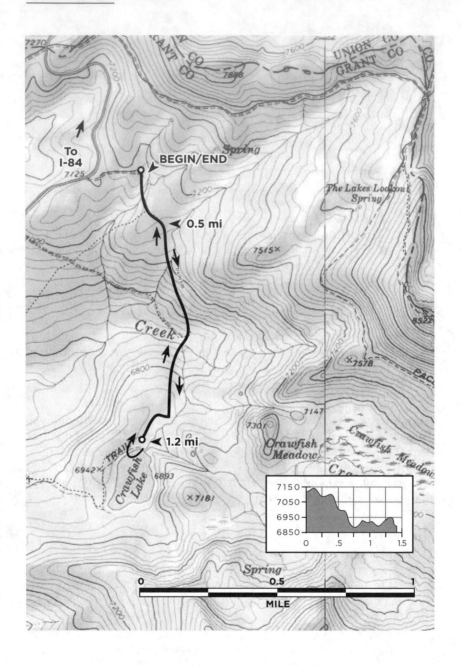

The Crawfish Lake trail climbs up from the lake.

cups Crawfish Lake. The lake is 1.2 miles from the trailhead, and you can follow a 0.5-mile trail around the lake.

GOING FARTHER

You can follow the Crawfish Lake Trail for another mile to a lower trailhead, which switches back and crosses an abandoned road several times before ending at the lower trailhead, located off Forest Road 73.

72. North Fork John Day Wilderness

RATING	🚶 🚶 🚶 🚶
DISTANCE	5.0 miles round-trip
HIKING TIME	3 hours
ELEVATION GAIN	350 feet
HIGH POINT	5,200 feet
EFFORT	Easy Walk
BEST SEASON	Summer
PERMITS/CONTACT	Northwest Forest Pass required/Umatilla National Forest, (541) 427-3231
MAPS	USGS Trout Meadows
NOTES	Leashed dogs welcome; good family hike

THE HIKE

This is a pleasant walk along a river on a National Recreation Trail that leads to the wild country of the North Fork John Day Wilderness.

GETTING THERE

Take exit 285 from Interstate 84 at North Powder and drive 28.5 miles via Country Road 101, Elkhorn Scenic Byway, and Forest Road 73 past the Anthony Lakes Ski Area to the North Fork Campground. The North Fork John Day Trail No. 3022 begins just beyond the campground entrance, 5,268 feet above sea level. GPS trailhead coordinates: N44°54,924′; W118°24.269′

THE TRAIL

This beautiful hike is popular with anglers and equestrians, and it is probably most populated in the fall during the hunting season. As a hiker, you'll probably appreciate the trail for one of the same reasons it's popular with hunters: there's plenty of wildlife along this route. Elk, bear, and deer are plentiful, and wolf sightings in the region have been confirmed. In any event, summer is probably the best time for this hike; if you decide to wait until cooler weather in the fall, it might be wise to wear bright colors—"hunter orange" is best—on your hike.

The trail meanders downstream from the North Fork Campground, following the north side of the river the entire distance. Begin by walking

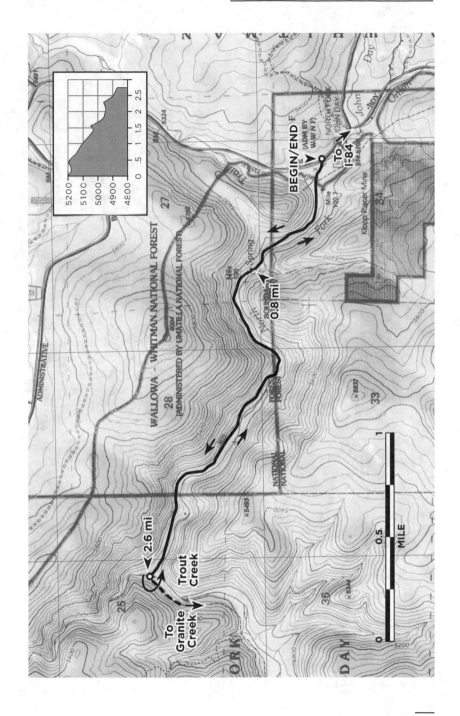

A footlog crosses a tributary to the North Fork John Day River.

west about 0.1 mile to the wilderness boundary, about 40 feet above the river. The path never strays far from the river, wandering through grassy meadows and an open forest of pine and fir. This country and the river were rich with gold and silver at one time, and the Klopp Placer Mine is located just south of the campground. You may see some miner's claims posted on trees along the route.

The trail descends along the riverbank, wandering through thickets of pine into more open forest with views to the river. At **0.8** mile, you'll pass a spring near the trail and look across the river to a creek tumbling from the placer mine. The path and river round a wide bend to the northwest and at **2.0** miles from the trailhead, turn west. Just beyond, you'll see a miner's cabin on river flats below, **2.4** miles from the trailhead. Continue another 0.2 mile to a crossing of Trout Creek, where there's a second miner's cabin. These cabins are private, but most owners allow public access and hope you'll respect their property.

GOING FARTHER
The North Fork John Day River Trail No. 3022 continues downstream for more than 13 miles, one-way. The path never leaves the river for any great distance, and there are few steep grades along the route. You can continue as far as your joints will allow.

73. Timothy Meadows

RATING	🚶 🚶
DISTANCE	5.4 miles round-trip
HIKING TIME	3 hours
ELEVATION GAIN	600 feet
HIGH POINT	5,900 feet
EFFORT	Moderate Workout
BEST SEASON	Fall, summer
PERMITS/CONTACT	Northwest Forest Pass required/Diamond Lake Visitor Center, (541) 793-3310
MAPS	USGS Mount Thielsen
NOTES	Leashed dogs welcome; equestrian trail

THE HIKE

This is a rewarding climb to a subalpine meadow below the stunning rock spire of 9,182-foot Mount Thielsen, one of Oregon's most impressive Cascade peaks.

GETTING THERE

From Oregon Highway 138 at Diamond Lake, turn west at the entrance to the Diamond Lake Resort and into the trailhead on the left, 5,410 feet above sea level. GPS trailhead coordinates: N43°11.010′; W122°07.994′

THE TRAIL

If possible, wait until the fall for this climb to a meadow with views of the jagged peak they call the "lightning rod of the Cascades," which—if you've watched an afternoon thunderstorm sweep across Diamond Lake—you'll agree is an accurate name. The meadows around the peak are damp in the summer and a breeding ground for billions of bugs, most of whom have sworn to the Great Godbug in the Sky to suck more blood from you than you'll find in two volumes of *Twilight*. The cool evenings of September and October discourage these nasty critters.

I might have rated this hike much higher, except for the fact that the first several hundred yards of path are shared with horses, and you'll likely wade through a lot of evidence of their passage. The trail winds to the east to an underpass of Highway 138; just past the highway, ignore a

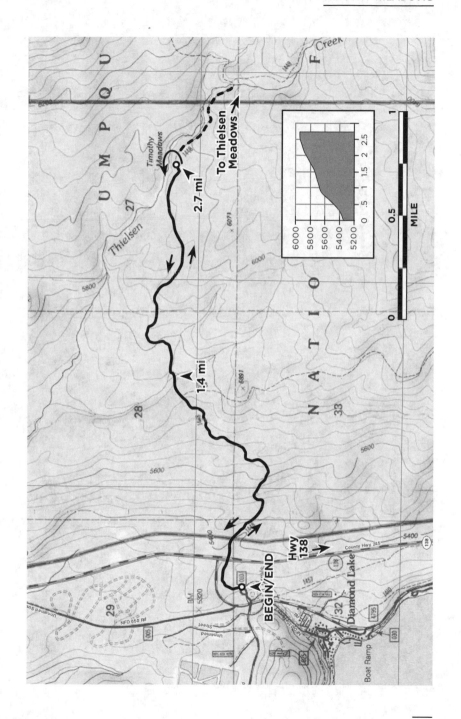

The wide Timothy Meadows trail is shared by equestrians near the trailhead.

couple of equestrian trails leading off to the left. You'll begin climbing in an open forest that provides peekaboo views of Diamond Lake below and Mount Bailey on the south side of the lake. The path climbs at a moderate and even grade, and **0.9** mile from the trailhead you'll find a junction with the Spruce Ridge Trail. Stay left at this junction and continue climbing, crossing a couple of seasonal creeks at **1.4** miles. You'll circle around a bluff and contour toward the east where the forest opens into grassy Timothy Meadows, a nice subalpine garden where Thielsen Creek winds out of the hills above. This is your turnaround point, **2.7** miles from the trailhead.

GOING FARTHER

You can climb to the end of Timothy Meadows for another 0.8 mile, one-way, to a junction with a trail leading to Howlock Meadows on the left. Keep right here and continue climbing along Thielsen Creek toward a junction with the Pacific Crest Trail No. 2000 in Thielsen Creek Meadows, 5.7 miles, one-way, from the trailhead.

74. John Dellenback Trail, Diamond Lake

RATING	🚶 🚶 🚶 🚶
DISTANCE	6.4 miles round-trip
HIKING TIME	3 hours 30 minutes
ELEVATION GAIN	75 feet
HIGH POINT	5,190 feet
EFFORT	Easy Walk
BEST SEASON	Fall
PERMITS/CONTACT	None/Diamond Lake Visitor Center, (541) 793-3310
MAPS	USGS Mount Thielsen
NOTES	Leashed dogs welcome; wheelchair accessible

THE HIKE

This paved trail around Diamond Lake yields great views of Mounts Thielsen and Bailey from the shore of a big subalpine lake.

GETTING THERE

From Oregon Highway 138 at Diamond Lake, turn west at the entrance to the Diamond Lake Resort and into the trailhead on the left, 5,300 feet above sea level. GPS trailhead coordinates: N43°11.010′; W122°07.994′

THE TRAIL

Here's another pathway named in honor of the late Oregon Congressman John R. Dellenback, who wrote legislation to establish the Oregon Dunes National Recreation Area (see hike #15 in this guide) and served as the director of the Peace Corps from 1975 to 1977. This paved route circles Diamond Lake and is used by bicyclists, joggers, and hikers. Cross-country skiers can use the trail in the winter.

The recommended portion of the trail begins at the Diamond Lake Resort and circles the north end of the lake to the Thielsen View Campground. You'll begin with a look at Mount Bailey across the lake and turn around at a great vista of Mount Thielsen. The trail follows the shoreline for most of the way, with very little grade. The first half-mile is managed as a barrier-free trail for those who do their hiking aboard a wheelchair.

In addition to the trailheads at the resort and Thielsen View Campground, you can start hiking from the South Shore Picnic Area or the

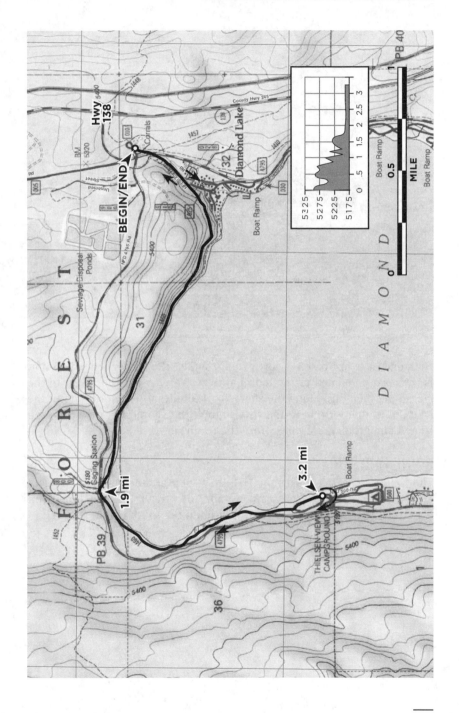

Mount Thielsen and Diamond Lake from the John Dellenback Trail.

Diamond Lake or Broken Arrow campgrounds. The recommended section is the least populated of the loop pathway. You'll walk southwest to the lakeshore, then turn along the shore for 1.9 miles to the north end of the lake. From there, circle to the south along the shoreline to the Thielsen View Campground, 3.2 miles from the trailhead.

GOING FARTHER

The Dellenback Trail makes an 11.1-mile loop around the lake. Beyond Thielsen View, the trail passes a number of private summer homes on leased forest property before circling around the south end of the lake.

75. Cleetwood Cove

RATING	🚶 🚶 🚶
DISTANCE	2.2 miles round-trip
HIKING TIME	3 hours
ELEVATION GAIN	700 feet
HIGH POINT	6,850 feet
EFFORT	Prepare to Perspire
BEST SEASON	Fall, summer
PERMITS/CONTACT	Entrance fee required/Crater Lake National Park, (541) 594-3000
MAPS	USGS Crater Lake National Park
NOTES	Dogs and bicycles prohibited

THE HIKE

This strenuous hike leads to the shore of Crater Lake. The view at the bottom isn't as great as the view at the trailhead, but it is the only way to catch a boat to Wizard Island.

GETTING THERE

From Oregon Highway 138, follow the North Entrance Road to Crater Lake National Park, where you'll be asked to pay an entrance fee ($10 per carload in 2009), then continue to the intersection with Rim Drive. Turn left and drive 4.5 miles to the Cleetwood Cove trailhead, 6,850 miles above sea level. GPS trailhead coordinates: N42.58.843′; W122º04.980′

THE TRAIL

It is easy, while you're looking down into that splendid blue water or across the immense crater created when Mount Mazama blew herself up, to forget that for every step you take downhill, you'll have to take one step uphill on the return. This is not a trail for folks who don't walk regularly or aren't accustomed to hiking steep trails, yet hundreds of visitors who aren't regular wilderness pedestrians make this trek every summer without incident. Lowlanders who hike sea level and river trails will almost certainly feel the effects of hiking uphill more than 6,000 feet above sea level. Simply be forewarned: This is no picnic in the park.

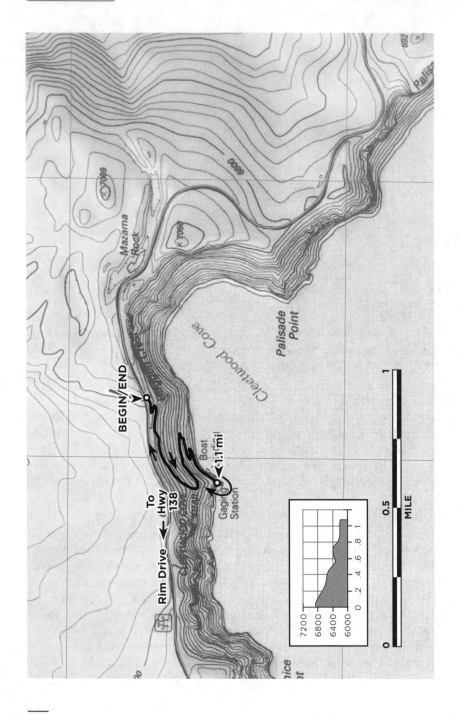

Crater Lake from Cleetwood Cove.

(Actually, it *can* be a picnic in the park if you tote your own food and drink.)

Before hitting the trail, decide if you'd like to ride a boat to Wizard Island, where there's a 2.5-mile round-trip climb to the island's crater. If that's your plan, buy a boat ticket at the trailhead parking area and get there early in the morning. If you're simply planning to take the only hike to the Crater Lake shore, lace up your boots and hit the trail. The advice about boots is not hyperbole; this is a rocky trail and sandals just won't do.

Begin by walking to the west down an evenly graded, wide trail that switches back in 0.1 mile and immediately turns back again to traverse down to a wide switchback about **0.5** mile from the trailhead. Continue down another 0.2 mile to another switchback and the boat landing. The shoreline here is very steep and there's little room for maneuvering, so after you've caught your breath and taken in the view, you can begin the tough climb back to the trailhead.

GOING FARTHER

If you've bought a ticket for the boat ride to Wizard Island, hop aboard the next boat and get off on the island, where you'll find a 1.2-mile trail, one-way, that climbs about 800 vertical feet to the crater.

76. Mount Scott

RATING	🚶 🚶 🚶 🚶 🚶
DISTANCE	5.0 miles round-trip
HIKING TIME	3 hours, 30 minutes
ELEVATION GAIN	1,250 feet
HIGH POINT	8,926 feet
EFFORT	Knee-Punishing
BEST SEASON	Fall, summer
PERMITS/CONTACT	Entrance fee required/Crater Lake National Park, (541) 594-3000
MAPS	USGS Crater Lake National Park
NOTES	Dogs and bicycles prohibited

THE HIKE

This is a tough climb to the summit of Crater Lake National Park and the best view in southern Oregon.

GETTING THERE

From Oregon Highway 138, follow the North Entrance Road to Crater Lake National Park, where you'll be asked to pay an entrance fee ($10 per carload in 2009), then continue to the intersection with Rim Drive. Turn left and drive past the Cleetwood Cove trailhead to a large switchback turn just before the Cloudcap intersection. The Mount Scott trailhead is at the parking area just around the switchback, 7,683 feet above sea level. GPS trailhead coordinates: N42°55.756′; W22°01.780′

THE TRAIL

Carry extra water on this hike and slather yourself in sunscreen, because the entire hike begins nearly a mile and a half above sea level and climbs from there. There's not a lot of atmosphere up here to block those nasty UV rays and—let's face it—you're going to be sucking half of it into your oxygen-starved lungs. This hike isn't nearly as steep as it's going to feel because of the lofty altitude. If you plan to take this trek, make certain you're in good shape and know the symptoms of the several forms of altitude sickness. My favorite—although B. B. Hardbody, my wife, disagrees

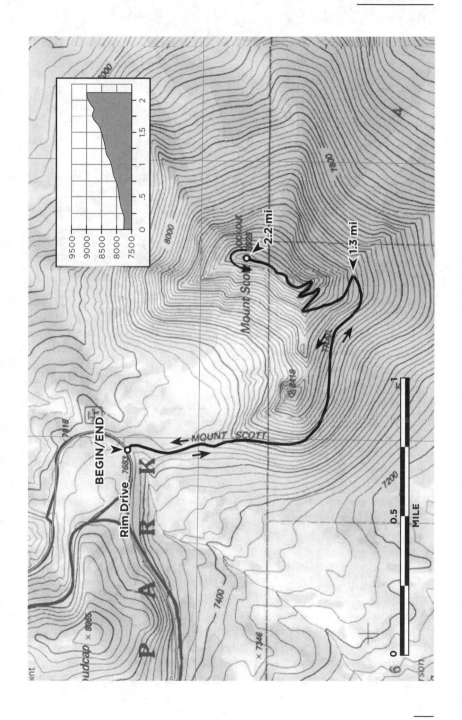

The trail to Mount Scott crosses a wide meadow and avalanche basin before climbing the peak.

violently—is HAFE, or High Altitude Flatulent Expulsion. No joke. You can look it up.

The hike begins with a gentle climb across a wide basin that you'd likely want to avoid in the winter, when avalanches clean the slope of trees, rocks, and the occasional unlucky cross-country skier or snow-shoer. You needn't worry unless some unthinking tourist at the summit, directly above, decides to roll rocks down the slope.

The trail leads due south for 0.3 mile before it begins to climb more steeply and turns to the east. The grade is steady and moderate but is likely to feel steeper because of the altitude. This is a good trail to practice the Real Mountain Climber's technique known as the "rest step." Essentially, you take one step uphill and transfer your weight to that foot, but leave your trailing foot on the ground momentarily, resting it before taking another step. I can modestly say that I am an expert at the rest step, so much so that Hardbody says I am practicing the "nap step." Big deal.

The open forest of pine and red fir opens gradually as you climb, passing several viewpoints where the forest is particularly thin. At 1.3 miles, you'll arrive at the first switchback, which announces a steeper grade for the remainder of the hike. The trail switches back again 0.4 mile beyond and leaves the forest behind completely. Switchback a couple more times before climbing directly up the sharp ridge 0.5 mile to the summit look-out. The building, balanced on the summit ridge, is usually closed to the public.

The view from the summit is more than impressive. To the north, you can see as far as the Three Sisters, Mount Jefferson, and, on a clear day, Mount Hood. Mount Shasta shines to the south and Crater Lake glistens below. Relax those quads, drink plenty of liquids, and nap step all the way home.

GOING FARTHER
Are you out of your freakin' mind? If you want more exercise, join the Marines.

McCall Park makes a loop trail with the Eastbank Esplanade in Portland.

URBAN TRAILS

Sometimes you just don't have the time to get away from the big—or even the little—city, but you'd still like to stretch your legs and get your glucosamine flowing to joints that need it. Thanks to City Mothers and Fathers and all the volunteers who make urban trails a reality, you can spend a morning or afternoon on a civilized pathway and still make that business meeting or get that roast in the oven.

Many cities and towns throughout Oregon serve up some sort of route intended exclusively for muscle-powered travel. They vary from gravel-surfaced single-tracks to smooth asphalt, from quarter-mile walkways to 20-mile supertrails along the Willamette or Columbia rivers. Following, from north to south along the Interstate 5 corridor, are four of the nicest urban pathways Oregon has to offer.

URBAN TRAILS

77. Eastbank Esplanade Loop, Portland

RATING   🚶 🚶 🚶 🚶
DISTANCE   3.7 miles round-trip
EFFORT   Stroll in the Park
BEST SEASON   Summer; open all year
SURFACE   Paved
NOTES   Joggers, strollers, bicyclists, leashed dogs welcome; downtown views and convenience

THE TRAIL

The Eastbank Esplanade–Tom McCall Waterfront Park loop is one of the nicest options for a post-conference stroll or brisk walk when you can't get away from the big city.

GETTING THERE

If you're walking, access to these waterfront walkways is most anywhere around the Esplanade near the Oregon Museum of Science and Industry, or across the river at Tom McCall Waterfront Park. If you're driving, the most likely spot to park is at the cul-de-sac on SE Caruthers Street.

THE WALK

The Vera Katz Eastbank Esplanade is a 1.5-mile promenade in the spirit of the Seaside Promenade, with a wide paved pathway that stretches north from the Hawthorne Bridge to the Steel Bridge spanning the Willamette River. If you've begun your walk near the Hawthorne Bridge, you'll first pass a number of interpretive signs that explain the effort to restore the river habitat and the history of the city's bridges. At 0.8 mile from the Hawthorne Bridge, the signs give way to four striking pieces of public art, including the *Echo Gate* under the Morrison Bridge, the *Ghost Ship* and *Stackstalk* on a concrete wall that was once part of a pier, and finally the *Alluvial Wall* to the south.

Beyond, you'll walk down a metal ramp to the left onto a floating walkway, 1.2 miles from the Hawthorne Bridge. It's 1,200 feet long and said to be the longest floating walkway in the United States. The walkway is nearly 18 feet wide and leads to the pedestrian/bicycle Steel Bridge. Cross the river here and turn north to walk along the river through Tom

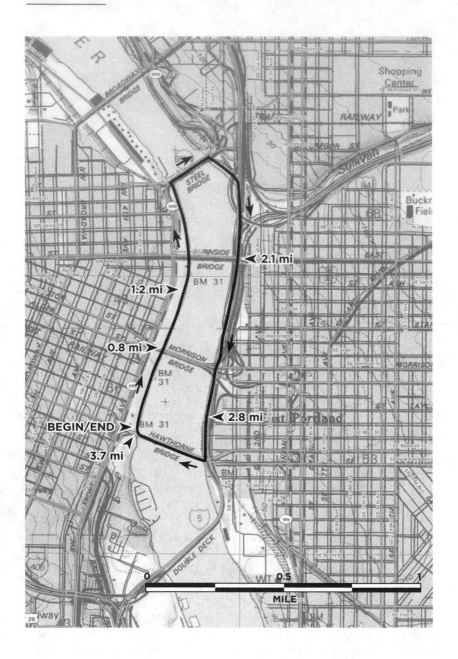

The Eastbank Esplanade Loop in Portland makes for one of the nicest in-city walks in Oregon.

McCall Waterfront Park, where a concrete bulkhead extends from the bridge back to the Hawthorne Bridge. You'll pass under the Burnside Bridge at **2.1** miles, where there's an outdoor market on weekends from April to December, and by the Salmon Street Fountain at **2.8** miles, a great playground for youngsters. Cross the Hawthorne Bridge and follow a ramp back to the Esplanade.

78. Minto-Brown Island Park, Salem

RATING	🚶 🚶 🚶
DISTANCE	5.0 miles round-trip
EFFORT	Stroll in the Park
BEST SEASON	Summer; open all year
SURFACE	Paved
NOTES	Joggers, strollers, inline skaters, bicyclists, wheelchairs welcome; muddy spots in winter

THE TRAIL

This is a great getaway into a portion of a 900-acre national wildlife refuge, practically in the middle of the city.

GETTING THERE

Follow Mission, Commercial, and Owens streets to South River Road and to the main park entrance, where you'll find at least two large parking areas. The city of Salem has also constructed the Minto-Brown Island Bikeway along South River Road to the park.

THE WALK

More than 20 miles of paved and dirt pathways can be found in the park, where you'll find lowland meadows, orchards, sloughs, and ponds. Two pathways, labeled A and B, meander through forest and along the Willamette River.

The recommended path follows the Willamette to the south for about 1.8 miles before turning inland through forests and fields for another 0.7 mile, then looping back and returning to the main parking area for a loop of **5.0** miles. The path features a number of side trails leading to wildlife observation decks by the river and ponds, as well as a paddleboat operation. The refuge is home to Canada geese and other waterfowl, and is a frog, toad, and snake paradise.

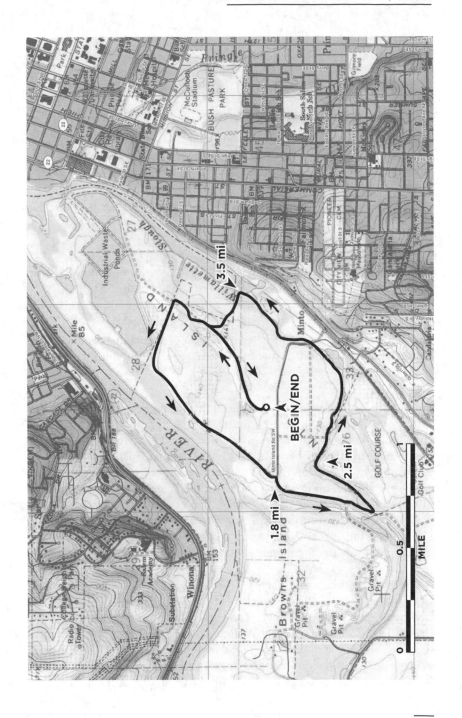

79. Riverfront Park, Corvallis

RATING	🚶 🚶 🚶
DISTANCE	6.4 miles round-trip
EFFORT	Easy Walk
BEST SEASON	Spring
SURFACE	Paved
NOTES	Multi-use bike path; off-leash dog section; great family outing

THE TRAIL

Here's an urban walk along the Willamette River with downtown biking and hiking retailers to tempt you to stray from the path.

GETTING THERE

Follow Oregon Highway 34 for 10 miles west of Interstate 5 to Riverfront Park. The north trailhead is just off Tyler Avenue in Corvallis.

THE WALK

This trek begins on a 12-foot-wide path that extends south along the Willamette River, passing three plazas used by groups for celebrations, community events, and a seasonal farmers market. You'll pass grassy areas and a number of benches for river-watching. Just across the river is the Oregon State University crew house and uptown, several of the city's hiking and biking shops. Decorative sculptures and a fountain attract pedestrians to the park.

At **0.8** mile, the trail passes a skate park, where you'll see a mess of youngsters and not-so-youngsters riding boards and BMX bikes, not always right side up. Picnic tables and benches make good viewing platforms.

The trail continues south across Mary's River and parallels Third Street to Crystal Lake Drive, where you'll turn and walk to the east. Pick up the trail again just south of Fischer Lane, then follow the path through the Crystal Lake Sports Park to the Willamette Park and Natural Area, where there's a Frisbee golf course and, in the natural area, an off-leash dog park. Willamette Park is the city's largest at 287 acres. The south end of the park is your turnaround point, **3.2** miles from the beginning of the path.

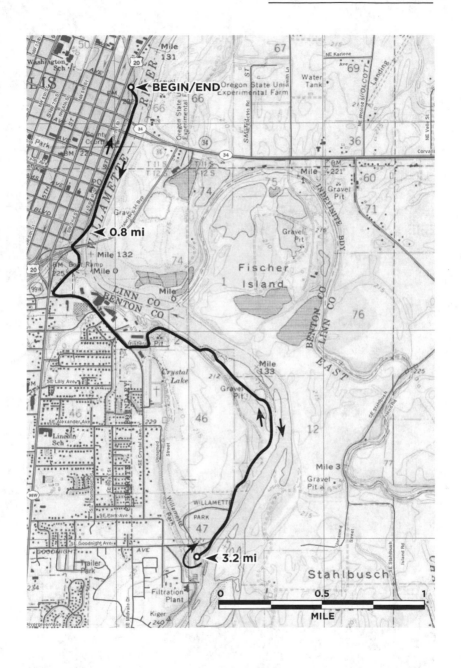

The Riverfront Park in Corvallis serves up a great urban walk.

80. Pre's Trail, Eugene

RATING	🚶
DISTANCE	3.4 miles round-trip
EFFORT	Stroll in the Park (walkers); Prepare to Perspire (joggers)
BEST SEASON	Summer; open all year
SURFACE	Wood chip; paved
NOTES	Historic jogging path

THE TRAIL

You can walk on this riverside path, but you run the risk of getting run down by joggers (actually, they're very courteous).

GETTING THERE

The three loops of Pre's Trail are located in Alton Baker Park, off Martin Luther King Jr. Boulevard in Eugene, just across the Willamette River from the University of Oregon campus.

THE WALK

Although you won't be ostracized for walking this pleasant path along the Willamette River, you might be more comfortable in a pair of Nikes. Wear sweats and walk at the side of the path, feigning a stitch in your side. Eugene is widely recognized as the birthplace of jogging and Pre's Trail is one of the favorite spots for doing just that.

The pathway is named for University of Oregon track star Steve Prefontaine, one of America's greatest distance runners, who met a tragic end in an auto accident in 1975. Prefontaine and his contemporaries are credited with popularizing running in America, and the University of Oregon is known for its success in track events, as well as being the alma mater of Phil Knight, the Nike shoe guy.

You'll find three main loops that constitute Pre's Trail. The southeast loop is **1.7** miles, the northwest is just over a mile long, and a center loop is **0.7** mile. The trails are part of a network of trails in Eugene and nearby Springfield. The longer of the loop trails is wood chip and bark, with portions of gravel and a short section of asphalt.

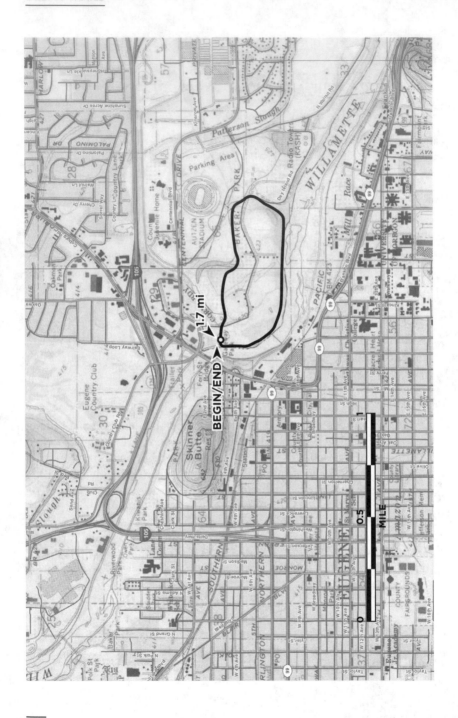

A jogger follows Pre's Trail in Eugene.

Index

Trail Notes

Trail Name: _____

Comments: _____

_____

_____ Rating: _____

Trail Name: _____

Comments: _____

_____

_____ Rating: _____

Trail Name: _____

Comments: _____

_____

_____ Rating: _____

Trail Name: _____

Comments: _____

_____

_____ Rating: _____

Trail Name: _____

Comments: _____

_____

_____ Rating: _____

Trail Name: _____

Comments: _____

_____

_____ Rating: _____

Trail Name: _____

Comments: _____

_____

_____ Rating: _____

Trail Name: _____

Comments: _____

_____

_____ Rating: _____

Trail Name: _____

Comments: _____

_____

_____ Rating: _____

Trail Name: _____

Comments: _____

_____

_____ Rating: _____

Trail Name: _____

Comments: _____

_____

_____ Rating: _____

Trail Name: _____

Comments: _____

_____

_____ Rating: _____

TRAIL NOTES

Trail Name: _____

Comments: _____

_____

_____ Rating: _____

Trail Name: _____

Comments: _____

_____

_____ Rating: _____

Trail Name: _____

Comments: _____

_____

_____ Rating: _____

Trail Name: _____

Comments: _____

_____

_____ Rating: _____

Trail Name: _____

Comments: _____

_____

_____ Rating: _____

Trail Name: _____

Comments: _____

_____

_____ Rating: _____

About the Author

As a youngster, Seabury Blair Jr. hiked, often lost, around the hills of his native Spokane, Washington. He continues to get lost, though with far greater skill after six decades of practice. The former outdoor editor of the *Bremerton Sun*, he emphatically denies the paper changed its name to the *Kitsap Sun* to disassociate itself from him. He is the author of *Day Hike! Olympic Peninsula*, *Day Hike! Columbia Gorge*, and *Backcountry Ski! Washington*. He and his wife, Marlene, reside near Spokane.

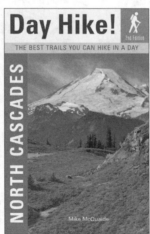
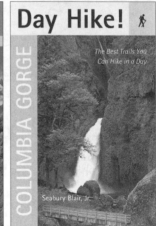